The Complete Guide to Writing Software User Manuals

# The Complete Guide To
# WRITING SOFTWARE USER MANUALS

Brad McGehee

Writer's
Digest
Books

Cincinnati, Ohio

**Library of Congress Cataloging in Publication Data**

McGehee, Brad M. (Brad Michael), 1957-
    The complete guide to writing software user manuals.
    Includes index.
    1. Electronic data processing documentation. 2. Technical writing. I. Title.
QA76.9.D6M34    1984        001.64'25        84-7235
ISBN 0-89879-138-3

*Design by Charleen Catt Lyon*

# Contents

**Preface**

**User Manuals Today** . . . . . . . . . . . . . . . . . . . . . . . . . . . . . . . . . . . . .1
User manuals—the bane of the computer industry. The benefits of good user manuals. Markets for manual writers and types of writers who write manuals. User manual basics: planning, determining your audience; manual organization; outlining, writing, illustrating and publishing the manual.
*Lawford & Associates: programmer David Lawford hires freelance writer Jill Bates to write the user manual for his original software, Home Mortgage Calculator.*

**Planning Your Manual** . . . . . . . . . . . . . . . . . . . . . . . . . . . . . . . . . . . .7
Planning the software and manual together—the advantages of collaboration. The planning process: defining objectives, establishing completion dates, determining the budget. Planning the manual after the software is written—gathering information about the software; the planning process.
*Lawford & Associates: David and Jill collaborate on initial planning for the Home Mortgage Calculator user manual, defining the manual's objectives, setting deadlines and establishing the production budget.*

**Your Manual's Audience** . . . . . . . . . . . . . . . . . . . . . . . . . . . . . . . . .14
Finding out about your audience: users' computer experience; knowledge of the application; what users hope to do with the program; understanding the program's terminology; the consequences of user error. Slanting the manual to a particular audience—beginner, intermediate and expert levels.
*Lawford & Associates: Jill researches the market for Home Mortgage Calculator in order to slant the manual to the users' level of computer expertise.*

**Manual Organization** . . . . . . . . . . . . . . . . . . . . . . . . . . . . . . . . . . . .21
The five factors in manual organization: logic, sequence, relevance, balance and consistency. Recommended manual organization: title page, copyright page, preface, table of contents, introduction, getting started, tutorial, reference section, appendix, glossary, index and quick reference card. When each element should be used, and what it should include.

*Lawford & Associates: Jill determines how the manual for Home Mortgage Calculator will be organized and which elements will be included.*

## Outlining Your Manual ...................................39
Before you outline: preliminary research—getting to know the software. Drafting the outline: deciding which sections the manual will have; developing a filing system to organize important information; determining major and minor subject headings; revising and editing the outline.
*Lawford & Associates: Jill familiarizes herself with the working version of Home Mortgage Calculator. Based on this knowledge, she prepares her outline for writing the manual.*

## Writing Style .........................................46
Establishing a point. Choosing the right words. Avoiding wordiness. Setting the right pace. Using examples and comparisons. Establishing tone. Using the proper voice and tense. Consistency. Grammar and punctuation. Reading your writing out loud.
*Lawford & Associates: Jill develops a style sheet to ensure consistency throughout the Home Mortgage Calculator manual, covering abbreviations, capitalization, jargon and terminology, numbers, punctuation and spelling. Readers are directed to additional sources of information on writing style.*

## How to Write Tutorials...................................57
Tutorials—the most important section of your manual. When to use tutorials. The novice-vs-expert dilemma. Guidelines for writing tutorials. Writing the tutorial segments. A complete sample tutorial segment.
*Lawford & Associates: In writing the first draft of the tutorial section for the Home Mortgage Calculator manual, Jill decides to include additional examples and exercises to help the beginning user gain confidence in the program.*

## How to Write Reference Sections .........................66
When to use reference sections. Two types of reference sections—dictionary-style and encyclopedia-style—and when to use each. Guidelines for writing reference sections. Four steps to writing ef-

fective reference sections.

*Lawford & Associates: Jill convinces David of the need for a reference section in the Home Mortgage Calculator manual, noting that expert users may prefer to skip the more detailed tutorial, that novices may need to refresh their knowledge of the program's operating features, and that software reviewers often check to see if a reference section is included with the manual.*

**Writing Your Manual from First Draft to Final Copy** ......73
Getting ready to write the manual. The tools you need to begin: the outline, the software and a compatible microcomputer, word processing software, and illustration supplies. The first draft of the manual for Home Mortgage Calculator. Rewriting the first draft. Testing the manual with potential users. Polishing the manuscript for style, grammar, and spelling. Proofreading the manuscript.

*Lawford & Associates: Jill writes the first draft of the Home Mortgage Calculator manual and revises it for testing with potential users. After testing is complete, she writes the polished version, incorporating the results of the testing. David approves the manual and gives the go-ahead for Jill to contract with a printer. Readers are directed to additional sources of information on word processing.*

**Home Mortgage Calculator User Manual**

**Illustrating Your Manual**................................112
Communicating with illustrations. Types of illustrations—screens and reports, tables and diagrams, and drawings—with examples of each. How to create illustrations—tools and techniques for creating your own. Working with freelance technical artists.

*Lawford & Associates: Jill notes in the Home Mortgage Calculator manual each place where an illustration is needed, including her guidelines for how the artist is to design and create each. Readers are directed to additional sources of information on technical illustration.*

**Designing Your Manual** ................................121
Principles of graphic design: unity, sequence, balance, proportion and emphasis. Designing the manual yourself—tools and techniques. Having the manual professionally designed—choosing and

working with a designer. What the designer does.

*Lawford & Associates: Jill convinces David that the manual for Home Mortgage Calculator should be designed by a professional designer, noting that a professional design will help sell the manual. They agree to include design services as part of the contract with the printer chosen to print the manual.*

**Printing Your Manual.....................135**
Types of printers: photocopy shops, quick-print shops and full-service printers. Deciding how to print and bind your manual. Self-designed and printed vs typeset; quick copy vs metal plate offset. Choosing a binding: spiral or loose-leaf. Business matters—dealing with your printer.

*Lawford & Associates: Jill prepares a bid form and gives it to six full-service printers. The lowest bidder has never printed a user manual before and has a reputation for missing deadlines, so she gives the remaining bids to David for a final decision. He decides on the next lowest bid, and Jill contracts with that printer to design and print the Home Mortgage Calculator user manual.*

**Copyrighting Your Manual .....................144**
Who owns the copyright—the manual author or software publisher. The copyright notice. Registering the copyright.

*Lawford & Associates: Although the copyright of the Home Mortgage Calculator user manual is to be in the company's name, it is Jill's job to complete the copyright registration form and register the copyright with the Library of Congress. The completed form is illustrated. Readers are directed to additional sources of information on copyright.*

**Freelance Manual Writing.....................150**
The freelance programmer as manual writer—why freelance programmers should write their own manuals, why they should not, and what they need to know. Collaborating with freelance writers. The freelance writer as manual writer—what kinds of work freelance writers can expect and where to find freelance manual writing jobs.

**Glossary .....................157**

**Index .....................162**

# Preface

Welcome to *The Complete Guide to Writing Software User Manuals*. If you have never written a user manual before, or if you have but want to increase your skill, this book is for you. Step by step, it teaches you how to write and produce manuals that are clear, understandable, and easy to use.

You can profit from this book whether you are a freelance writer, freelance or in-house programmer, or in-house manual writer. If you are a freelance writer who has never written a user manual before, you will learn a new skill that will open many new opportunities for writing assignments. If you are a programmer or in-house manual writer, learning to improve the quality of your manuals translates into happier customers and perhaps increased sales.

The book uses many examples and illustrations to show you how to improve your manuals. At the end of each chapter is a fictional account of a software firm, Lawford & Associates, that has decided to come out with a new software product called Home Mortgage Calculator. You will follow the progress of Lawford & Associates as it goes about having a manual written for this program, from initial planning all the way to the final printed manual, which is printed in its entirety in Chapter 9.

The most important topics covered in this book are:
- How to Plan the Manual (Chapter 2)
- How to Determine the Manual's Audience (Chapter 3)
- How to Organize the Manual (Chapter 4)
- How to Outline the Manual (Chapter 5)
- How to Write the Manual (Chapters 6-9)
- How to Illustrate the Manual (Chapter 10)
- How to Publish the Manual (Chapters 11-13)
- How to be a Freelancer (Chapter 14)

Reading this book is your first step to writing and producing better software user manuals.

I want to thank Paul Jenner and Bob Berndt, professors at Southwest Missouri State University, who contributed their expertise to the sample manual in Chapter 9. I also want to thank my editor, Robert Lutz, without whose efforts this book would not have been published.

# 1. User Manuals Today

**User Manuals: The Bane of the Computer Industry**

Software user manuals are in a sorry state today because manual writers usually do not take the time to tailor the manual's writing to the needs of its users. Assuming the reader has some background in computer use and terminology is a fatal mistake in many manuals. For example, which of these passages is easier to read and more understandable?

**A.** Input the text source file into the text editor (be sure it is in the standard ASCII format) by giving the Load command. This function is implemented by the LDFILE.EXE program residing on the program disk. Once the source file has been loaded, you are ready to execute the editing commands.

**B.** Before you can begin editing and making changes in your letter, you must first load it into your computer. Here's how.

**Step 1:** On the video display screen you should see the 'Main Menu.' (See figure.) If you don't, repeat the instructions found on page 14, step 5.

**Step 2:** To load your letter, first press the 'L' key. Within two seconds the video display screen changes and asks you to type in the name you gave the letter in lesson number three.

**Step 3:** Now type in the name of the letter and press the ENTER Key. After about four seconds your letter is loaded into the computer and should now be displayed on the video display screen.

Believe it or not, the two passages above say the same thing. The first passage not only assumes that the user understands all the terminology, it also lacks any form of organization, rendering its message unclear. Only a few devoted computer "hackers" might be able to figure out what is being said. Most users would find the prose unbearable to read and probably wouldn't be able to learn from it how to use the program.

The second example, though much longer, is clearly organized and very readable. While some terms may not be readily understandable to you because they are out of context, they would be clear to the user, having been defined earlier in the text. Unlike the first passage, the second is not open to misunderstanding. Everything is laid out step by step. At the very least, this is what good software manuals are all about.

**Benefits of Good User Manuals**

Writing and publishing a good user manual is expensive, so why go to all the trouble? In any business venture you have to spend money to make money. This is true for the software publishing industry as well; the better the manual that accompanies the software, the more advantages that accrue. Some of these benefits are:

1. If a manual is designed to be easy to use for all readers, the number of potential customers for the software package is increased and the result is sales. Many manuals, because they are not written with beginners in mind, artificially limit their potential sales because they shut out novice users.

2. A well-written and well-designed manual makes the software itself stand out from the crowd. Many potential software customers make their decision about what package to buy after browsing through several at a store. If your manual outshines the rest, the odds are in your favor that the customer will buy your software package over another.

3. Comprehensive and easy-to-use manuals reduce the amount of after-sale support required of dealers and publishers. Dealers prefer to carry software that requires little support, and so they tend to stock software packages with excellent manuals. Also, good manuals reduce the number of technical support personnel publishers have to hire, a big money saver.

4. A good manual that is liked by the customer is often spoken highly of. This is word-of-mouth advertising you can't buy; business software, in particular, is especially dependent on good word-of-mouth, and an attractive, readable manual can only help.

5. When software is reviewed in magazines and books, a good portion of the review is usually devoted to a program's manual, specifically describing what is good and bad about it. With the proliferation of reviews, and the weight many computer users put on them, it is wise to write a good manual to increase the chances for a good review. Some new programs' success or failure is based on the reviews they get. Good reviews also establish "name-brand recognition" for your product—especially important if you expect to publish a line of products.

6. Being able to claim you have a quality manual is becoming a significant sales point in product advertising.

**The Market For Manual Writers**

Today there are thousands of software publishers publishing tens of thousands of software packages. According to one industry source, over 250 new software programs are released each month, each requiring a user manual.

Not only is the demand for new manuals exploding, there is a need for the rewriting of older manuals. When microcomputer software first came into existence in the late 1970s, many of the users were hobbyists who did not demand easy-to-use manuals. Today, however, the largest number of users are computer novices who demand clearly written manuals. These older manuals have to be rewritten if the publishers hope to maintain a share of the growing microcomputer software market.

Because most of the software publishers are small operations, the industry's biggest need is for freelance writers who contract for one job at a time, either writing new manuals or rewriting older ones. The larger publishers usually hire in-house manual writers although freelancers are often used, especially for overflow work.

Chapter 14 (Freelance Manual Writing) takes an in-depth look at the business aspects of freelance programmers and writers who write software user manuals.

## The Manual Writer

There are many different types of manual writers, and to eliminate confusion in this book, they are all grouped together under the heading of manual writer. As a reader of this book, you probably fit into one of the following categories:

1. *Freelance writers*, either those specializing in user manuals or those doing other writing as well. They are hired by software publishers or freelance programmers, on a contract basis, to write and sometimes to handle the publishing of manuals.

2. *In-house or freelance programmers* who write the user manuals for the software that they write. The in-house programmer may be expected to write the user manual because he's the expert on the program, or because the publisher cannot afford to hire a manual writer. The freelance programmer usually cannot afford to hire out the manual writing (unless he collaborates with a freelance writer for a share of the royalties), so he must do it himself.

3. *In-house writers* who devote all their time working with programmers to write user manuals. Depending on the publisher they work for, they may also be responsible for designing the manual and having it published. In-house writers often start out as programmers and end up as full-time writers, or they are writers who have no computer experience and are trained on the job.

No matter where you fit in as a manual writer, the information in this book will help you write better software user manuals.

## User Manual Basics

There are certain basic steps that you must take whether you are writing a book, novel, magazine article, or user manual. Each of these steps is described in one or more chapters in this book. With user manuals in mind, these steps include:

**Planning.** (Chapter 2) Before you can begin writing, your first step is to establish the objectives of the manual and set out a plan to implement them. This provides the road map you need to guide you along the path to a successful manual.

**Determining Your Audience.** (Chapter 3) Before you can write your manual to meet the needs of the user, you first must determine who the user is going to be. This knowledge allows you to slant the manual's content, organization, and writing style appropriately. The better the fit between the manual and user, the more understandable and easy to use it will be.

**Manual Organization.** (Chapter 4) The fundamentals of

manual organization—logic, sequence, relevance, balance, and consistency—all contribute to the clarity of a manual. Each of these considerations must work together to enlighten your particular audience about the program's use and operation.

**Outlining the Manual.** (Chapter 5) Once the audience has been identified and an appropriate organization determined, the actual outlining of the manual begins. You start by researching the use and operation of the program, and continue through several drafts of the outline, each becoming more detailed, until you have included all the important aspects of the program. This outline is the guide that you will follow to write the actual manual.

**Writing the Manual.** (Chapters 6-9) Once you learn the fundamentals of good manual writing style (Chapter 6), and how to write tutorials and reference sections (Chapters 7 and 8), you can write the first draft (Chapter 9). For most manual writers, this is probably the most overwhelming part of writing, but it is actually only a small part of the writing process. After the first draft comes the second draft, where you will work on the manual's content and organization. Then comes a testing period (called *beta-testing*) to verify the manual's ease of use and completeness. This testing is usually done along with the beta-testing of the software itself. After testing, a final, polished draft is completed, ready to go to the printer.

**Illustrating the Manual.** (Chapter 10) Illustrations not only add variety to a manual and make it more interesting, they facilitate the learning process for the user. Although you cannot be expected to provide professional quality illustrations for your manual, you can decide what is needed and provide rough drawings so a professional artist can finish them.

**Publishing the Manual.** (Chapters 11-13) As a manual writer, you may or may not have anything to do with getting the manual published. If you do, you must understand that this aspect may be as important as writing clear text. The graphic design, the printing, and the copyrighting of the manual are all important parts of publishing a manual.

### Lawford & Associates

To help you gain a better understanding of the manual-writing process, let's consider a fictional account of how a programmer/writer team writes a user manual—from program concept to completion of the software package. At the end of each chapter in this book we will follow the production process of a software publisher, Lawford & Associates, as the manual is written for the program, Home Mortgage Calculator. Although this account will illustrate only one way a manual might be written, the principles covered here apply to most manual-writing situations.

David Lawford, owner and senior programmer of Lawford & Associates, a small software publishing company, has decided to design and write a program called Home Mortgage Calculator. On the basis of some marketing research he commissioned from a local college, he sees a need for a program that calculates the various financial aspects of home mortgages and that is targeted toward beginning users. In essence, the program will perform these functions:

**1.** Calculate any one of the following amounts, assuming the rest are known: house purchase price, percentage down payment, loan term, annual interest rate, monthly mortgage payment.

**2.** Compare what monthly mortgage payments would be at various interest rates and purchase prices.

**3.** Compare what monthly mortgage payments would be at various interest rates and loan terms.

Because Lawford & Associates is a small software publisher without any in-house writing staff, David decides to hire a freelance writer to write the user manual for Home Mortgage Calculator. He wants to get the manual writer involved early in the planning of the program so that the writer can contribute his or her expertise to the program's design and can learn the program as it is written, so the manual can be completed sooner.

Through a friend at another software publisher, David learns of a freelance writer, Jill Bates, who has previously written two manuals. He invites her to his office to discuss her writing of the manual.

Jill tells David about her experience and shows him copies of her previous work. She says that she is putting the final touches on a book on word processing but that she should be done in about two weeks and will be available then to start a new project.

Satisfied with Jill's background, David negotiates with her and they sign a contract. (See Figure 1-1.)

## 1. Author's Responsibility

Author agrees to perform the following work:

(a) Develop plan to meet objectives (established by the publisher) of the user manual for the computer program: Home Mortgage Calculator.

(b) Develop detailed outline of manual.

(c) Complete a preliminary draft of the manual for use during the beta-testing of Home Mortgage Calculator.

(d) Complete a final draft of the manual for Home Mortgage Calculator, incorporating the results of the beta-testing.

(e) Assume responsibility for having the manual published, including researching appropriate printers and copyrighting the manual.

Author also agrees that each step described above must be approved by the Publisher before the next step is to take place. Also, Author agrees to attend weekly meetings, each Monday at 1:00 p.m., starting with the first Monday in February, until the manual is complete.

## 2. Time Schedule

Publisher and Author agree to work together to establish the exact date of the completion of work. These dates are directly related to the progress toward completion of the program: Home Mortgage Calculator. At the very latest, the manual should be complete by May 15, 1984.

## 3. Ownership of Copyright

The Publisher retains all ownership rights to the manuscript, and the Author agrees to copyright the manual for the Publisher, in the Publisher's name.

## 4. Payment to Author

For the work described above, the Publisher agrees to pay the Author the sum of $3,500.00. An advance of $500.00 is to be paid at the signing of this contract, and the remaining $3,000.00 is to be paid in three payments of $1,000.00 each, on the following dates: February 1, 1984; March 1, 1984; and April 1, 1984. If additional work is requested of the Author that is not described in this contract, the Publisher agrees to pay the Author $20.00 per hour.

**Figure 1-1**
**Agreement**

*This agreement dated the 3rd day of January, 1984, between Lawford & Associates, Box 4585, Springfield, MO 65808 (Publisher), and Jill Bates, 123 S. Mentor, Springfield, MO 65807 (Author).*

*Figure 1-1 is only a sample contract between the fictional characters of Lawford & Associates and Jill Bates. You should always seek the advice of an attorney before signing any contract.*

# 2. Planning Your Manual

Every successful new business devises a business plan before it opens its doors. Essentially, a business plan is a detailed proposal stating the business's objectives—what it intends to produce, how much it hopes to sell, how it intends to produce the product, and so on—and most important, exactly how the business hopes to implement the plan—where it will buy the raw material, how many people it will hire, what media it will advertise in, and so on. A business plan is not written overnight but assembled and refined over weeks or months after consultation with many people who have expertise.

A software manual requires the same kind of careful planning. First you must establish the objectives of the manual and second you must develop a program to implement those objectives. Ideally, the manual writer and the programmer should sit down before the program is even written and together establish the manual plan. (The program plan is beyond the scope of this book.)

The first part of this chapter discusses this suggested method. The second part considers the possibility that the manual is not planned or started until the program itself is completed. Although not the best way to plan a manual, more often than not it is the way most manuals are actually written, usually because of the software publisher's lack of foresight.

**Planning Software and Manual Together**

Planning at its best is a cooperative effort among many people. Each person brings to the planning process his own unique viewpoints and insights, each contributing what he knows best. After all, nobody has the knowledge and experience to know all aspects about every proposed project. Another benefit of cooperative planning is that different aspects of the project can be coordinated among the various people involved in it. This factor is especially important in a software development project in which the programming and manual writing duties are separated.

The benefits of early cooperation between the programmer and the manual writer include:
•   While programmers are expert in program design and writing, they are usually not expert communicators. This shortcoming often results in programs that are unnecessarily difficult to operate. The writer, with expertise in communication, can often make suggestions to improve a program's ease of use, adding to its usefulness and success.

• Cooperative planning ensures that what the user learns from the manual corresponds exactly to what the software will do. This eliminates any possibility of confusing the reader as he reads the manual for the first time, learning how to use the program.

• Early planning allows the manual writer to begin writing earlier in the product development stage and helps to get the software package on the market sooner. This time advantage often gives the software a competitive edge over similar products.

• Cooperative planning allows the manual writer to help establish both the objectives and the way they will be implemented. The manual writer should not have format, deadlines, or budgets forced on him, but should contribute to the decisions. The manual writer who takes part of the responsibility for the success of the manual is likely to be motivated to do a better job.

• For the freelance writer, planning ensures that the client understands and approves what you will be doing.

Cooperative planning also implies a good working relationship between the programmer and manual writer. To this end, clearly defined job responsibilities are essential. Whether the writer is on staff or freelance, the exact duties of the writer and programmer should be spelled out in detail, either in a contract or in the plan itself. Doing this helps to prevent any misunderstandings about what is expected from each. If the writer does not know that it's his responsibility to coordinate the testing of the manual after it's written, problems are likely to result when testing begins. Communication flows more easily if each knows his respective responsibilities.

Once the duties have been established, there must be an open line of communication between the programmer and the writer. This is usually not a problem if they both work at the same location, but it can present difficulties for the freelance writer working at home or another location. Regular meetings and phone access are important so the writer can ask the programmer questions about the program's operation. The lines of communication should be established early in the planning stage.

Cooperative planning should be both challenging and rewarding for the programmer and manual writer. Anything less may affect the final outcome of the software and manual and result in a defective product.

**The Planning Process**

The planning of software and manual will differ from project to project, depending on the program's use and audience. Although the specifics of planning change, however, the overall process remains the same. The following is one way the planning of a manual may be done, but it is not the only way. Use it as a guide for your own planning.

The first step in planning any manual is to establish its goals or objectives. These are the things you want your manual to accomplish with resounding success. A brainstorming session among everybody concerned with the software package should be held, with all the possible objectives being discussed until the most important and final ones are decided on. As part of the formal plan, the objectives must be written down for the record and as a basis later to determine the means to implement them.

Some of the possible objectives that the manual writer and publisher might establish while planning the manual (the objectives of the software are beyond the scope of this book) include the following:

**1.** To enhance the sales of the software. Good manuals usually receive good reviews, helping spread the word about the software; and potential customers are often swayed from one program over another because of better manuals.

**2.** To explain to the user clearly and accurately the use and operation of the program. Such an explanation also contributes to the success of the software and reduces the need for customer support.

**3.** To complete various stages of the project by agreed-upon dates. The different steps such as outlining, preliminary draft, manual testing, final draft, and printing should all have clearly established completion dates. A schedule allows the program's marketing to be carried out efficiently.

**4.** To accomplish the writing and printing of the manual within a specified budget. The cost of the manual affects the profitability of a software project and must be controlled.

The above are only a few of the objectives that might be considered in the writing of a manual. Once they have been established, the next step is to determine how to implement the objectives. Unlike the objectives, the details are usually determined by those people expert in the relevant areas. Because the writer is the expert, he should establish the details in consultation with his supervisor. Like objectives, the details should be formally written so that they can act as a guideline to the various stages of producing the manual.

To show you some of the different details that must be determined in a manual plan, here are some relating to the above objectives.

• **Enhanced Sales.** To meet this objective, many actions could be taken, such as the following: (1) hiring marketing consultants to evaluate the current software market and determine how the manual could be designed to be most effective; (2) examining the manuals of competitors to see how they can be outdone; (3) conducting research to see what readers want in a good software manual.

• **Clear Instruction.** The best way to implement this objective is to be sure that the manual's organization, writing style, and format follow generally accepted principles of effective communication. It's a good idea to develop a style manual to ensure consistency. Also, to verify the clarity of the instructions once the manual is written, testing should be done.

- **Completion Dates.** A formal schedule should be established for each step in the writing process along with a method to verify that the writing is being completed as scheduled, as well as a schedule for client approval at each stage in the writing process.
- **Budget.** Developing the budget for a manual is probably the most difficult of all planning details. This is so because a budget takes into account many kinds of costs and many people, such as printers, have to be contacted in order to arrive at the estimated costs. While this can be done by the manual writer, you might consider seeking the aid of an accountant or printing production professional for suggestions on how to proceed.

These are just a few of the details that have to be determined to carry out your manual's objectives. As you can see, planning can take considerable time. Don't think you can overlook planning just because your manual is small. A plan not only organizes the writing of a manual, but helps to control the outcome. As each stage is completed, it should be checked off. From time to time, the plan should also be reevaluated to see that everything is going according to schedule, and if it is not, the plan should be changed to meet unexpected occurrences. Planning is a dynamic process that continues throughout manual writing.

## Planning the Manual after the Software Is Written

Unfortunately, manuals often are not planned along with the software. This often happens when the programmer does not give the user manual much weight in the software package. The programmer might lack insight or may be trying to keep costs down or to save time. Many programmers think that manuals can be written in a couple of days. If you are called in as a writer on such a project, you may not have much time to plan the manual and you will probably have many things imposed on you that you cannot change. You can only hope to do your best to change the mind of the programmer and produce the best manual you can given the limitations of the situation.

### Gathering Information

Unlike the manual writer who plans the manual along with the software and who learns the use and operation of the program from the very beginning, you must learn the program from scratch. You can't hope to plan the manual, and later outline and write it, unless you know it intimately. Once you know the program, you can begin planning the objectives and their implementation. The best strategy for learning the program is as follows:

- Read the program documentation provided by the programmer, assuming any exists. Program documentation includes the flowchart of the program's logic, a description of the equipment the program operates on, the programmer's notes on program operation, software specifications, and a variety of other odds and ends. Examine them carefully to get what you can from this information and use it as a basis for interviewing the programmer. If you are unfamiliar with computers and this is your first user manual, you should consider taking seminars or classes on microcomputers. Many are offered by computer stores and community colleges. Such a course will provide the foundation you need to understand the program documentation. See Chapter 14 for more information about what you have to know to write software manuals.

• Interview the programmer about the general nature of the program and how it works. Take a lot of notes and ask about any special features that may not have been covered by the program documentation. Often a programmer takes some important aspects of a program for granted and does not write them down.

• Use the program yourself, trying out everything it is supposed to do, pushing it to its limits. Take notes at all times, keeping track of how the program reacts in all cases, leaving nothing unexamined. You will probably encounter problems as you go along, so be sure to get the questions answered by the programmer as they arise. If possible, try to borrow a microcomputer (if you don't already have one) so that you can bring it to your place of work. In this way you will be able to learn the program at your own pace.

• If possible, talk with other people who have used the program—people who have tested it using a preliminary manual would be ideal. If the manual was formally beta-tested, get a copy of the results. Incorporate all this information into your notes.

Once you have the program mastered, both on beginning and expert levels, you are ready to plan the writing of the manual.

**The Planning Process**
Your steps here are more limited than if you had planned the manual with the software, because many of the objectives, and some of the details of how the manual is to be done, will be imposed on you. For example, you may be told the manual must be completed in three weeks, including printing. Your plan will probably be established by yourself and for your own benefit.

As before, you need to establish your objectives for the manual. They of course differ with the program, the audience, and your imposed constraints. Your major objective should be to have the manual instruct clearly. Marketing, time schedule, and budget goals may already be imposed, so you need only follow them.

Once you have established your goals and written them down (writing them down helps to clarify your thoughts), work out your method for implementing them given your constraints. Plan out, step by step, how you intend to accomplish the manual writing, writing each step down so you can later check your progress against the plan.

Later, as you are writing the manual, you will constantly have to reevaluate the plan, modifying it to reflect current needs. The best advice you can have when faced with such a situation is to try to convince the programmer of his folly in not getting you involved earlier, and let him know that as a result you need to suggest some changes in your work in order to make the manual the best it can be. On rare occasions you might give up the chance to write a manual if the writing conditions are so bad that you cannot do a job you would be proud of.

## Lawford & Associates

Two weeks after signing the contract, David Lawford and Jill Bates meet for their first weekly, Monday meeting. This is the first of many meetings to plan and monitor the writing of the user manual for Home Mortgage Calculator.

"I want to start this meeting by telling you about the objectives and plan I have outlined for the Home Mortgage Calculator program," said David. "Just ask questions as I talk about the program. If you have any suggestions, just interrupt me."

For the next hour David outlines how Home Mortgage Calculator will work and shows Jill rough sketches of the program's screens and reports. As David explains, Jill takes detailed notes and often interrupts him with questions about why certain user commands are planned as they are.

Most of Jill's questions center around the program's main menu. David's plan calls for a main menu that has an option to call up two additional menus to use the major features of the program.

"It seems to me," said Jill, "that the user wastes a lot of time and may even be confused by three separate menus in such a small program. Couldn't you combine the three menus into one, saving the user the effort of going from menu to menu and reducing the possibility of confusing the user?"

"With some additional work, sure, Jill. But it would add about two weeks to the schedule and I'm not sure if the extra effort is worth it."

"Pardon the sarcasm, but you sound just like a programmer. You think too much in terms of what's easiest for you and not what's best for the user. When you hired me, you said you wanted this program to be operated by anybody. If you really mean that, you're going to have to emphasize program ease of use a little more."

"I know how you feel, Jill, but I have to face realities. My company is small and I can't afford the extra time spent programming. My budget is just too small."

"Yes, but what is more costly to you, two weeks of extra work or publishing a software package that won't sell?"

"Well, you're the expert on communication. I know you're right; I was just hoping to save some time. Okay, I'll go with the one menu idea. Now that you know more about the program, let's discuss the objectives of the manual."

For the next hour and a half David and Jill discuss the major objectives of writing the manual and some of the possible ways they can be implemented. Tentatively, they agree on the following major objectives:

1. Manual must be easy for beginners to use.
2. Manual must clearly communicate the operation of the program.
3. Manual should help sell the software.
4. Manual should be printed and ready to distribute within three months.
5. The initial printing is to be 5,000 copies within a printing budget of $10,000.

Two and a half hours after the meeting began, David ends the meeting. "Jill, besides making suggestions on the program, have the plans to carry out the manual's objectives ready by next Monday. Start from what we discussed today and go from there. Use your expertise to fill in the blanks. We'll discuss what you come up with next week and I'll make a final decision on your ideas then. See you Monday."

# 3. Your Manual's Audience

One of the advantages radio advertising has over television advertising is that advertisers can better target their commercial messages to specific audiences. Western clothing stores advertise on country and western stations, stereo stores advertise on rock stations, and drug stores advertise on easy listening stations. Advertising that is targeted to specific individuals is effective because it is tailored to prospective customers' needs.

The same is true for software user manuals. The more carefully a manual is tailored to fit the needs of its audience, the more effective it is in getting across its message. While this might seem easy, this is where most user manuals fail. The manual writer fails to identify who the potential audience is and neglects to slant the manual's contents to fit the needs of that audience. The result is a manual that is at best confusing, and at worst, worthless.

A manual's scope, its actual content, must be written from the user's perspective. We can see this more easily if we break down a manual's content into two different aspects: breadth and depth.

Breadth of content has to do with what topics are covered in the manual. For example, a beginning computer user does not care if the software is written in BASIC or if he can make modifications to the program. A computer expert, on the other hand, might find this information useful, maybe even necessary. When slanting the breadth of a manual to a particular audience, you include those topics that are appropriate for the user of the program.

Depth of content has to do with the degree of detail that is covered in the manual. A beginning user needs to know exactly how to make a backup diskette of the program diskette that comes in the software package. This instruction may include details as to what steps have to be taken, along with illustrations to show how to insert a diskette. A computer expert, though, would not need so much detail; most likely, a statement to the effect that a backup diskette should be made is enough. He has made many backups before and doesn't need remedial instruction. When slanting the depth of a manual to a particular audience, include detail, or remove detail, as necessary to meet the needs of the user.

Why go to all this trouble? If a user wants to learn a program badly enough, won't he make the effort to read the manual, no matter how it is written? This is not the point. Your job as a manual writer is to clearly communicate the use and operation of a program. Psychological research has shown that learning is enhanced, and information retained longer, if information is presented in terms that are familiar to the user.* Writing a manual from the user's perspective eliminates hindrances to learning. After all, if your manual cannot be understood by the user, the program cannot be used to its full potential, if at all, and the manual fails to achieve its purpose. Before you begin planning and writing a manual, take the time to find out who will be using your program.

This chapter is devoted to learning how to slant a manual's content to meet the needs of its audience. However, this is not the only way to slant the manual to the audience. The chapters on manual organization and writing style will also explain how to tailor your writing to communicate better with the user.

## Finding Out About Your Audience

Before you can slant your manual's content to match your audience, you must learn who that audience will be. This information should be provided to the writer by the programmer. If you are the programmer, then you should have conducted appropriate research before you began planning and designing your program. (The marketing research techniques used to determine potential audiences are beyond the scope of this book.) Whether or not you began planning the manual along with the program planning, the audience for the program should at least have been determined. If it was not, the program is bound for trouble.

To learn who your audience is, you should get the following information. If the programmer cannot provide it, you may have to conduct informal research on your own to ensure a proper slant. This research could consist of discussing the matter with people who are in a position to have special insight or knowledge of the program, such as programmers, computer users, and employees of computer stores. Following is a partial list of information you need to have, along with examples of how you might slant the manual to particular audiences:

• **Users' computer experience:** Will the users be beginners, intermediates, experts, or all three? The answer to this question will determine how you will handle the breadth and depth of the manual's contents. Manuals aimed at beginners have to include more introductory information, whereas expert users will need more technical data.

• **Knowledge of application:** How well will the users know the use or application of the software? What is their experience with a database, if that's what the program involves? A word processor?

---

*See these articles from the anthology *The Psychology of Written Communications*, edited by James Hartley (Kogan Page, 1980): "The Facilitation of Meaningful Verbal Learning in the Classroom" by David P. Ausabel, p. 17; "Just Fill In This Form: A Review for Designers" by Patricia Wright & Philip Barnard, p. 173.

An accounting system? If the user is unfamiliar with the application, you may have to include introductory information describing the many uses of the software and how to get the most from it, in addition to the information telling the user how to operate the software.

• **What users hope to do with the program:** What will the various users hope to accomplish with the program? If the program is a word processor, will they be typing short letters, manuscripts, statistical reports? If they will be using the software mainly to write short letters, then the examples you use in the manual should emphasize how to write short letters. If users will be using the program to type statistical reports, then your examples must show exactly how to do this. Only when you know what the program will be used for will you be able to tailor the manual's examples to meet the needs of the users.

• **Understanding of the program's terminology:** Do "balance sheet" and "income statement" mean the same thing to users? Will they know the difference between a "computer file" and a "file cabinet"? The users' knowledge of computer terms will affect what terms you use in your writing and how you will go about introducing and explaining them as they come up in the text.

• **Consequence of user error:** If the user enters an incorrect entry or accidentally erases data, how will this error affect the user? How many dollars or how much time will a particular error cost the user? If a particular procedure of using the program can be potentially dangerous to important data, you must include in the manual a warning to this effect and present the procedure in such a way as to reduce the chance that any user error can occur. The greater the chance for error, the more effort you must devote to preventing it from occurring by including all necessary information.

The answers to each of these questions will affect the way you should slant the content of the manual. To make this task easier, write out the answers on separate sheets of paper and keep them handy. Along with the answers, write out the implications of each and indicate how you intend to slant your manual to meet the needs of your audience. You will find this procedure helps to clarify your thoughts about the manual and will be of great benefit later when you write the outline.

**Slanting to a Particular Audience**

There are thousands of possible combinations of potential audiences, each with their unique needs. It would be impossible to offer specific guidelines for each combination. To give you some idea of how a manual can be slanted to different audiences, the following guidelines focus on two of the above questions about audiences: the amount of the users' computer experience, and the users' knowledge of the application. To refine the audience further, each question is divided into three degrees of experience.

## Computer Experience

Probably the most important information you need about your manual's audience is their level of computer knowledge and experience. One of the main reasons manuals do not communicate clearly is that they assume the user knows more than he does. To prevent this problem, you must identify the level of the users' knowledge and slant the breadth and depth of the manual's content to match. Use the following guidelines to help you.

**Beginner.** Computer beginners have little or no experience or knowledge about computers. They don't understand the concepts or terminology, or even the extent of what a computer can do for them. Therefore, not only must the program's use and operation be explained, but so must everything from turning the computer on to inserting a cassette into a cassette player and a diskette into a disk drive. From a breadth standpoint, all related topics must be covered. You can't assume the user knows anything. The amount of depth must also be comprehensive, detailing every possible step. Always assume the user will make every possible mistake, and write the manual to help the user avoid such mistakes or correct them easily when they happen.

**Intermediate.** The intermediate user either owns his own microcomputer or uses one at work or school. He knows about the hardware, so the breadth of the manual should concentrate on the use and operation of the program. Tutorial (step-by-step, how-to information) material should concentrate on the unique aspects of the program, encompassing its breadth. Such important aspects as disk preparation and backup probably don't need detailed explanation, nor do common terms need to be defined. There should be a strong reference section (how-to information arranged for easy access) so that the user can skip the tutorial section if he feels he

**Expert.** An expert computer user knows all the technical aspects, how they work, and probably two or more programming languages. He is interested only in this particular program and not about computers in general. A tutorial may be helpful for complex or unique programs, but the expert user prefers reference material, as it is faster to read and assimilate. The breadth should cover technical aspects about the program, such as how to write custom printer drivers or whether it is possible to write assembly language routines to speed up the operation of the program. While these technical aspects should be given in great depth, the general usage information need not be covered in detail.

## Knowledge of Application

After the computer experience of the user, the user's knowledge of the application is most important to the slant of a manual. Even an experienced user may never have used an electronic spreadsheet and so may need basic training. Or, an accountant may know all about general ledgers but may never have operated a computer.

When you slant your manual, you must consider both the user's computer knowledge and his knowledge of the application.

To help you slant your manual to fit the application knowledge of the user, here are some guidelines.

**Beginner.** Beginners, who know little or nothing about the software application, must be introduced to the basic concepts, terminology, uses, and operation of the software. Depending on the complexity of the program, it might be appropriate to have a special section in the manual explaining the basics of how the application works. A separate tutorial would provide hands-on experience. The breadth of either section would have to cover all possible user needs, with complete details of the application as the user is learning it for the first time.

**Intermediate.** Intermediate users have used similar applications and understand what they do and the general operating principles. The basic thrust of the manual is to teach them the operation of this particular application. For example, suppose they know what a word processor is and most likely have used other such programs. Your job is to teach them how to use this particular software package. Sophisticated programs still require a tutorial approach, but a strong reference section is beneficial for those who think they can forgo the tutorial. The actual operation of the program is stressed for this user.

**Expert.** The expert has probably programmed similar applications before and understands them completely. He wants to know how this one is different from other similar programs and how he can modify it to meet his needs. The breadth must cover technical features and provide any necessary information for patching or altering the program. A strong reference section is important because many expert users dislike to wade through tutorials; they would prefer scanning a well-prepared reference section, to learn about the program much more quickly.

**Lawford & Associates**

After her meeting with David Lawford, Jill begins to work at home on the plan to meet the objectives outlined in the meeting. The first three objectives (making the manual easy to use, communicating clearly, and helping sell the software) raise two big questions in Jill's mind that were not discussed in detail at the meeting: Who is the audience for the software and manual? How should the manual be slanted to fit the needs of the audience? Before Jill can write a detailed plan, she feels she must answer these questions.

To start this line of inquiry, she gets out five sheets of paper and at the top of each one writes one of the following questions:
- What is the users' level of experience with microcomputers?
- How familiar are the users with home mortgage calculations? Do they even know what they can do with such a program?
- How will the users go about using the program? Will they buy it

only if they are planning to purchase a house and use it once, or will they purchase it because they think they may have some future use for it and want to familiarize themselves with the application?

•   How well do the users understand the jargon of computers and of home mortgage calculations?

• Will user errors present great problems to the user if they occur? How much do errors cost in lost time?

Jill feels that once these questions are answered, she will have the background she needs on the audience to be able to slant the manual so that it meets the objectives.

From the information she received in talking to David and reading the marketing report prepared by his consultant, she is able to answer most of the questions about the audience. She puts this information on the sheets of paper where she has written the five questions. Even after doing this, however, she is still not clear on the level of the experience the users will have. She calls David.

"David, this is Jill. I have a question about the program's audience I'm not clear on."

"Go ahead, I'm listening."

"The question concerns the level of computer experience the user will have. Should I assume that the typical user is a complete novice, needing detailed instructions about the computer besides the program, or will he have a basic understanding of computers?"

"They will have at least a basic understanding of computers. Go ahead and assume that the users have read their equipment manuals and understand them, but don't assume much more. I'm afraid that if we assume less, our manual would be too long and would only repeat what is already in the computer's operator manual."

"I'm glad you mentioned that. I'm going to have to borrow an IBM PC from you along with its manuals so I can familiarize myself with it. My Apple won't run Home Mortgage Calculator. When do you think I can get one?"

Having gotten her main question answered, Jill goes on to other business with David.

Now possessing all the information she needs to know about her audience, Jill uses the same five sheets of paper to write out how she plans to slant the manual. Here is how Jill answered each of the five questions about the manual's audience and how she intends to slant the manual to meet the needs of the audience.

•   **What is the user's level of microcomputer experience?** Assume user is a beginner but does have a basic understanding of how to operate his own computer. Whenever hardware-related instruction is needed in manual, assume user understands basic terms and procedures (e.g., DOS operating system, how to insert a diskette), but detail step by step exactly how to use the program in relation to the hardware (e.g., how to make backups using Home Mortgage Calculator).

•   **How familiar are users with the application of Home Mort-**

gage Calculator? The consultant's research indicates most of the users will understand the basic concepts behind home mortgage calculations and don't need a lesson in them. This means that a separate section explaining how home mortgage calculations work is unnecessary. Only the particular way Home Mortgage Calculator handles the calculations need be covered.

• **Who will be using the program, and how?** The marketing study stated that most of the purchasers would buy Home Mortgage Calculator for home use. It also suggested that the program would be heavily used immediately when purchased, and then on other occasions, separated by months or years. This implies that the user would need a good tutorial to learn the basics of the program the first time, and a good reference section to be used at later times just to refresh his memory.

• **How well does the user understand the terminology of computers and of home mortgage calculations?** Because the user is considered a beginner in computers but knows how home mortgage calculations work, terms unique to the program must be defined early in the text, but more common terms can be left to the glossary.

• **Will user errors cause problems?** Because the program is relatively simple, and data can't be destroyed by improper use, there is little need to take extra effort in warning the user to be careful.

With this information, Jill is now prepared to begin planning the actual manual, listing what must be done and in what order, to meet each of the objectives.

# 4. Manual Organization

Imagine the confusion resulting if a telephone book were organized by ascending phone numbers, or a software directory were organized alphabetically by the names of the publishers, or a novel started with the climax. Each of these publications would lose much of its usefulness. Every type of written communication has its most logical and appropriate form of organization. This is especially true for software user manuals.

Manual organization is the arrangement of necessary operating information about a software product into a functional, orderly whole. When you organize your manual, you must take into consideration the following factors.

• **Logic.** The organization must make sense to the user. For example, do not confuse the user by interjecting into the introduction a way to speed up the operation of the program by altering the program itself. Introductions are supposed to introduce, not provide detailed technical information. Each organizational element of a manual (discussed in detail later) has a specific purpose.

• **Sequence.** Factual material should be ordered in a way that meets the needs of the users; the exact sequencing depends on the type of material. For example, tutorials (see Chapter 7) should start chronologically (preparing the working copy of the software, loading the software into the computer, and so on), and continue step by step, progressing until the end (ending the session, turning the computer off). Reference sections (see Chapter 8), on the other hand, can be grouped by similarity of topic or organized into alphabetical order.

• **Relevance.** Include only related or pertinent information that applies to your particular audience. For example, do not tell the user how the program was designed if the program is targeted toward the school/educational audience.

• **Balance.** The amount of factual material should not vary excessively from one operating feature of the software to another. Likewise, do not shortchange an important subject because you happen to think most users will not use the feature or because you're just feeling lazy.

• **Consistency.** Each organizational section or subsection must be consistent with every other section. Use the same format and same names of operations in each section. For example, don't use a format of introduction, body, and summary in one section of the tutorial and then use only the body in the next.

Organization is important because it gives structure to a manual. A good structure makes the manual easy to use and enhances its clarity. Clarity, of course, is the essence of good communication. Benefits of good organization for the user include:

• Organization into logical parts breaks the manual into small, easily "digestible" portions that do not overwhelm the user. This format enhances the user's learning of the material.

• A clear structure prevents a manual from being psychologically threatening. This point is especially important to adult users who are not used to learning new subjects.

• Sound organization makes it easier for the user to find the information he needs, enhancing his ease of learning and satisfaction with the software package.

• Separate sections allow experienced computer users to skip sections that are not relevant to them, allowing them the option to devise their own approach to reading the manual and learning the software. Many experienced users don't like to be forced to read everything in a manual; they are interested only in the actual operation of the software, not the preliminaries.

Not only does clear organization aid the user, it also helps the manual writer. It provides the framework you need to begin writing the manual. Many writers get bogged down in their writing because they have little idea where they're going. This problem is usually a result of their not taking the time to plan their writing. Once you understand the basic organization of a manual, however, you will have the framework to begin your outline (discussed in Chapter 5).

## Recommended Manual Organization

There are many different ways to organize a software user manual. The organization you select must be based on your expected audience and the type of software product you are writing about. To help you choose an appropriate organization, the rest of this chapter is devoted to a description and discussion of the various options. The organizational elements covered are the following:

• Title Page
• Copyright Page
• Preface
• Table of Contents
• Introduction
• Getting Started
• Tutorial
• Reference Section
• Appendix
• Glossary
• Index
• Quick Reference Card

In the following sections you will learn the purpose and benefits of each of these organizational elements, as well as when to use them, what to include in them, and how to write them. In addition to the information on tutorials and reference sections in this chapter, there is a separate chapter devoted to each for a complete discussion of how to write these critical sections.

As you read about the various organizational elements, try to understand each so that you can decide which ones apply to your situation. Only you are familiar enough with the software product and its audience to know what structure will best meet the needs of its users.

## Title Page

### Purpose
The title page is the psychological beginning of a manual and is expected by most users. It introduces the manual and should be designed with marketing in mind.

### When to Use
The title page should be incorporated into all manuals. Small manuals might combine the title page with the front cover.

### What to Include
The title of the software, a phrase or statement indicating that the manual is a user manual, and the name of the publisher should be included on the title page. Optionally, you might include the names of the program and manual writers and perhaps illustrations that complement the content of the manual. (See Figure 4-1.)

### How to Write
The title page normally is the first right-hand page the reader sees after the cover is opened. Title pages can be strictly functional, listing the necessary information centered on the page, or can be graphically designed to make the page more visually appealing. Your budget and the available time will affect your decision. See Chapter 11 for the benefits of using good graphic design throughout a manual.

## Copyright Page

### Purpose
Like the title page, the copyright page is expected by the user. Essentially, it is an extension of the title page, presenting additional information about the manual.

### When to Use
Always use a copyright page with manuals that have a title page.

### What to Include
The copyright page should always have the copyright notice and copyright infringement warning. See Chapter 13 for additional in-

formation. You can also include the name and address of the publisher; the names of the program author, manual author, and manual designer; other acknowledgments; and other miscellaneous business matters like customer service information and software copyright notice and warranty. (See Figure 4-2.)

**Figure 4-1**
**Title Page**
*The title page of your manual can be as simple as this one, or can be formally designed by a professional artist. The form of the title page is more of a marketing decision than an "ease-of-use" decision.*

# ELECTRONIC ENCYCLOPEDIA USER MANUAL

### Visionary Software Corporation

**How to Write**
The copyright page should always be the page immediately following the title page, on the left-hand side of the manual's binding fold.
Like the title page, the copyright page can be strictly functional,
with all information left-hand justified (that is, all text flush against
the left-hand margin), or it can be graphically designed to fit the design of the manual.

**Figure 4-2
Copyright Page**

*Like the title page, the
copyright page may be
graphically designed with
marketing aspects in mind.
If you are a freelance
writer, you will probably be
told what has to go on the
copyright page.*

## CUSTOMER SERVICE

If you ever experience any problems with
this program, please call our toll-free
customer service phone number.

Customer Service Phone Number
(800)123-4567 Weekdays
9:00 a.m.-5:00 p.m.

First Edition, April 1984
(C) 1984 Visionary Software Corporation
All Rights Reserved

Visionary Software Corporation
Box 4585
Springfield, MO 65808

Program Written by Fred Lutz
Manual Written by Sara Achabal

**Preface**

## Purpose

Often the preface of a manual is the first part that is read by prospective purchasers and owners of the software. For this reason, the preface should give a brief overview of the software and should act as a sales tool. From the overview, the prospective customer knows what the software does and can make an informed buying decision. Once the software is purchased, the preface is usually read again, and it should provide a broad foundation that orients the user to the rest of the manual and the software.

## Benefits

- A preface makes a good first impression. Prospective customers will assume that the rest of the manual is as well organized.
- Prospective customers will not have to flip through the manual to find important information.
- Because the prospective customer can get an overall impression of the program quickly, store sales personnel should not have to spend as much time covering basic aspects about the software.

## When to Use

A preface should always accompany a software user manual. Smaller manuals might combine the preface with the manual's introduction, described later.

## What to Include

In your preface, assume the user knows absolutely nothing about the software or about computers. If the user does not understand something you say, he might be turned off from buying the product.

　　You should try to:

- Welcome the user.
- State the purpose of the program.
- State the intended audience.
- List the features of the program.
- List the benefits to the prospective customer.
- List the computer equipment required to operate the program.
- Describe the potential of the program. For example, if the program allows the user one thousand accounting transactions per accounting period, mention this capability. Do this with as few technical terms as possible.
- Describe the outline of the manual.

　　With all of this information gathered in one place, the prospective customer will have the information he needs to make a purchase decision.

## How to Write

The preface should be highly structured, with headings that direct the user's attention to important points, short introductory sections to each important point, and indented areas with graphic devices like bullets to emphasize important details. Sentences should be direct and brief. (See sample preface in Figure 4-3.)

The length of a preface depends on the complexity of the software. As a rule of thumb, two to four pages is recommended. It should not be so long and packed with information as to overwhelm the user.

The preface usually is located between the copyright page and the table of contents. You can see a complete sample preface in Chapter 9.

**Figure 4-3**
**Preface**
*This partial preface is from the fictional program Electronic Encyclopedia.*

---

**Preface**

Welcome to Electronic Encyclopedia.
Electronic Encyclopedia is the first complete, computer-based encyclopedia. As with a conventional encyclopedia, you can look up thousands of articles on every conceivable subject. Electronic Encyclopedia is intended for any computer owner who wants the speed and flexibility of computerized information retrieval.

With Electronic Encyclopedia, you can:
• Retrieve articles on over 10,000 different subjects. Each article varies in length from 200 to over 5,000 words, covering each subject in complete detail.
• Search subjects using any combination of search words you want. For example, you can search for "lions," "lions and tigers," "lions and Africa," "lions and zoos," "lions or tigers," and so on. Only the subjects you choose will be displayed on the computer screen.
• Compile your research information into one separate location to be used for research of any kind.
• Print portions or complete articles.

Electronic Encyclopedia's benefits include:
• Fast retrieval of information. Instead of wasting time thumbing through a conventional encyclopedia, you can request any subject and it will be displayed on the screen within three seconds.

**Table of Contents**

## Purpose
The table of contents is the user's road map to finding his way about the user manual. The user should be able to get a quick overview of the manual and discover what needs to be done to get the software to work.

## Benefits
- It gives potential customers an overall view of the content and organization of the manual. If well done, it should inspire the user's confidence in both the manual and the software.
- It provides the user with quick access to important information.
- It allows the experienced computer user to skip sections that may be repetitive.
- It saves you, the manual writer, from receiving embarrassing software reviews if you don't include one.

## When to Use
The table of contents is mandatory in every manual, no matter what its size.

## What to Include
All major sections and subsections to be included in the manual itself must also be included in the table of contents with relevant page numbers.

## How to Write
There are two major ways you can write a table of contents. Each will be discussed separately.

**Standard Table of Contents.** The standard table of contents is what is found in most nonfiction books and software manuals. It immediately follows the preface and lists the contents, first by section, then by subsection, all with page numbers. (See Figure 4-4.) Its use is appropriate for all short and many long manuals. Sometimes with long manuals, however, this type of table can extend over four or more pages, so it is somewhat hard to find what the user needs quickly because everything is lost in the mass of information.

**Summary Table of Contents.** The summary table of contents is more appropriate for long, complex manuals. Instead of listing each major section with the subsections listed directly below, this format lists only the major sections, accompanied by a short summary of the information found in the section. Once the user finds the correct chapter, he is referred to a section's (or chapter's) individual table of contents found at its beginning.

A section's table of contents breaks the section down into the various subsections, allowing the user to go to the correct page. (See Figure 4-5.) Splitting up the table of contents helps to create the illusion that the manual is not as complicated as it really is. The

Writing Software User Manuals

front table of contents acts as a general directory and the sectional table of contents guides the user more specifically.

Whichever method you choose to use in your manual, keep in mind that the format should be readable and fit into the overall graphic design of the manual.

**Figure 4-4**
**Standard Table of Contents**

## Table of Contents
## Electronic Encyclopedia

**1. INTRODUCTION**
Section Overview .............................................. 3
Why You Should Read This Manual ......................... 3
How to Use This Manual..................................... 4
Following Examples........................................... 5
Words You May Not Know ................................... 7
How This Program Works ................................... 10
How to Cope with Error Messages.......................... 18
Summary ..................................................... 21

**2. GETTING STARTED**
What You Need to Get Started ............................. 22
Preparing the Program Diskette............................ 24
Making Backup Copies....................................... 27

**3. TUTORIAL**
Introduction.................................................. 30
How to Use the Tutorial..................................... 31
Loading the Program......................................... 32
The Main Menu............................................... 35
Entering the Search Word ................................... 39
Using "and" in the Search.................................. 46
Using "or" in the Search ................................... 50
Using "not" in the Search .................................. 54
Saving the Search........................................... 58
Printing the Search Report ................................. 61
Leaving the Program......................................... 68

**4. REFERENCE**
Introduction.................................................. 71
How to Use the Reference Section.......................... 72
"And" Command.............................................. 74
Entering the Search Word ................................... 76
Leaving the Program......................................... 81
Loading the Program......................................... 83
Main Menu................................................... 87
"Or" Command ............................................... 94
"Not" Command ............................................. 96
Printing the Search Report ................................. 98
Saving the Search Report ..................................100

**5. APPENDIX: Error Messages** ............................104

**6. GLOSSARY** ............................................109

**7. INDEX** ...............................................112

Don't wait until the last moment to write the table of contents. Of course, you won't know the exact page numbers in advance, but the table of contents should be one of the first sections you write when you complete the manual's outline. This step is discussed in detail in Chapter 5.

**Figure 4-5**
**Summary Table of Contents**
**Electronic Encyclopedia**

## Table of Contents

**1. INTRODUCTION** . . . . . . . . . . . . . . . . . . . . . . . . . . . . . . . . . . . . . . . .   3
You are introduced to the manual and the overall operation of the program.

**2. GETTING STARTED.** . . . . . . . . . . . . . . . . . . . . . . . . . . . . . . . . .  22
You learn what equipment is required to use the program and how to prepare the program diskette for use.

**3. TUTORIAL.** . . . . . . . . . . . . . . . . . . . . . . . . . . . . . . . . . . . . . . . . .  30
Step by step, you learn the operation of this program from loading the program, to searching, to exiting the program.

**4. REFERENCE** . . . . . . . . . . . . . . . . . . . . . . . . . . . . . . . . . . . . . . .  71
The reference section allows you to look up any feature of this program. All topics are arranged in alphabetical order for your convenience.

**5. APPENDIX: Error Messages** . . . . . . . . . . . . . . . . . . . . . . . . . . . .104
All your questions about error messages are answered in this appendix.

**6. GLOSSARY** . . . . . . . . . . . . . . . . . . . . . . . . . . . . . . . . . . . . . . . . .109
Terms unique to this program as well as common microcomputer terms are covered.

**7. INDEX** . . . . . . . . . . . . . . . . . . . . . . . . . . . . . . . . . . . . . . . . . . . .112

# Introduction

## Purpose
The introduction is a more detailed overview of the software and manual. It provides the broad concepts of how the software works and lays the foundation for the remaining sections.

## Benefits
- An introduction gives the user a sense of direction and purpose.
- An understanding of the broad concepts right away inspires the user's confidence that he can operate the program without problems.
- The introduction groups all introductory information into one convenient, logical section.

## When to Use
An introduction is always mandatory but may be combined with the preface in a small manual.

## What to Include
To make it easy for you to see the many possible parts of an introduction, this section is broken down into several parts which can serve as a guide.

**Introduction.** Begin the introduction section with a quick overview. As briefly as possible, tell the user what is coming up in this section, tell why it is important, and list all the major topics that will be covered.

**Why You Should Read This Manual.** In this section, you should try to convince the user that it is important for him to read the manual. Be brief and persuasive. Write no less than one sentence and no more than one paragraph and list the benefits as you see them for your particular manual. For example, your main argument might be that the user will get better use out of the software and have fewer problems when the manual's instructions are followed closely.

Including this section also benefits you and the software publisher by eliminating misunderstandings by the user, creating a happier customer and one who requires less customer support.

**How to Use This Manual.** This section tells the user how to get the most out of the manual. Step by step, you should lead the user through each section, briefly explaining each and telling why it is important to the user and how he can best take advantage of it.

The length of this section depends on the size and complexity of the manual. Many small manuals may need only one paragraph to cover this topic completely.

**Following Examples.** If your manual has many examples or exercises that may be misinterpreted, you will want to show the user how to follow them properly. This explanation reduces the chance that the user will be confused and enhances his understanding of the program.

Step by step, introduce the user to any particular notation you use in examples and exercises. Include screens, reports, and any other illustrations necessary to explain procedures.

**Words You May Not Know.** If you feel that some of the terms you will be using in your manual may not be understood by the user, perhaps because they are unique to the program, take the time to define them now before he gets into the manual's tutorial and reference section. This precaution reduces the possibility of misinterpretation and minimizes the amount of page flipping the user has to do to check out words in the glossary. The more experienced and knowledgeable the user is, the less need for this section.

Start this section with a brief introduction explaining why it is included. Then immediately define the terms, one by one, alphabetically. It is safer to include too many words than too few. In some cases you might want to include an example of how the term is used.

**Program Overview.** The program overview explains what the program does and the functional concepts behind the way it works. It provides the foundation the user needs before he begins the tutorial. With some very complex software, such as database managers or word processors, it is a good idea to explain the general concepts of how the software works, especially if the users are beginners. Benefits that accrue to the user from reading an overview include:

• A broad overview of the program now orients the user to the details that will follow in the tutorial.
• With complex software, users are often uncertain whether they can master it. Learning fundamentals first, before delving into details, increases the confidence of the user.
• Presenting overview information before detail information reduces the chance that the user will misunderstand details given in the tutorial.

An overview introducing fundamental concepts should be included in all manuals. The length will vary according to the user's experience and the complexity of the program.

Start this section by explaining what is coming and why the information is important. Next, explain what the program does for the user. Then go into an explanation of the general operating procedures of the program. Ignore details that may confuse the user at this early point and use illustrations where appropriate.

**Program Control.** Here you explain any significant keyboard commands that are used by the program. You will thus familiarize the user with common keyboard commands and save yourself from discussing them in the tutorial, where you should be concentrating on more important details. You also reduce the chance that users will become confused about what keyboard commands do. This is an important point, as many different programs use the same key for completely different functions. The completeness of your description and the number of keys explained will depend on your audience.

**How to Cope With Error Messages.** Before the user begins any hands-on use of a program, you must explain to him how to handle errors if they should occur. Errors of any type, human or computer, can be exasperating to the user. If users know ahead of time what to expect, they will be more psychologically prepared to deal with errors if and when they occur.

Include this section in all manuals. As there is no software that is error-free, you must tell users how to handle all possible error situations. Begin this section with an explanation of what is to follow and tell why it is important. Then explain what an error message is, how to recognize one, and what to do about one.

**Summary.** The summary reviews the highlights of the introduction section and (1) puts in one place a summarization of all that was just read, helping the user grasp the material; (2) reinforces the important points just learned; and (3) acts as a reference if the user later wants a quick review of the section.

In most cases, use a summary only if your introduction is longer than six or eight pages. An introduction shorter than this is usually not difficult for the user to grasp and remember.

Usually, this summary lists the highlights of the introduction, point by point, using some graphic device such as bullets to aid a quick reading of the summary.

See Chapter 9 for a comprehensive example of an introduction.

## Getting Started

### Purpose
The getting started section walks the user through the procedures necessary to prepare the program (and possibly computer equipment) for use.

### Benefits
- It eliminates potential user problems by stating exactly what steps need to be taken to prepare a working copy of a program.
- This is the first place in the manual where the user sits in front of his computer to follow instructions. If the user finds this step easy to accomplish, he will be confident that he can complete the rest of the manual successfully.

### When to Use
In any manual, always include a list of the necessary computer hardware and software required to make the software operational. In all cases where the user has to prepare a working copy of a program, include the step by step procedures. In the case of software packages that come with a diskette already prepared, this portion of this section can be left out of the manual.

### How to Write

Start with an introduction that tells the user what the section contains and why it is important. Next, list in detail the exact computer hardware and software required to make the program work. Break down the equipment list into required equipment, optional equipment, and other necessary items, such as paper or specially printed forms. Also mention any other printed material the user may need to have on hand, such as hardware, operating system, or language manuals. In some cases, you'll also need to specify the kind of input data the user will need and in what form.

After all the necessary items are listed, lead the user step by step through the preparation process. The experience level of your audience will determine how detailed the steps should be. For example, beginning users should be led from the inserting of diskettes to turning on the computer. Programs designed for experienced users may skip the basic fundamentals and concentrate on the unique aspects of the program's operation.

## Tutorial

### Purpose

The tutorial is the core of the user manual. Step by step, the tutorial teaches the user the concepts and operation of the software. It does this by introducing one concept at a time and employing examples and exercises to reinforce what is taught.

### Benefits

- Because the tutorial breaks down concepts and operations into single ideas, one at a time, the user is not overwhelmed by the material and learns one point before going on to the next.
- The user is walked through the learning process so he does not feel left on his own to learn the material.
- Examples and exercises are given to provide actual experience and familiarity with the software. Answers are given so that the user knows that he is doing well.

### When to Use

In general, tutorials should be included with most programs. The only exceptions might be simple games and utility programs targeted toward experienced users. The depth and comprehensiveness of the tutorial is directly proportionate to the experience of the user.

### How to Write

See Chapter 7 for an in-depth look at how to write tutorials.

## Reference Section

### Purpose

For large manuals, a reference section is a quick place to seek out detailed information about the use of the software. It collects all the pertinent information into one easy-to-use location.

### Benefits

When the user needs an in-depth look at some part of a program, he can go to the appropriate reference section instead of hunting all over the tutorial section to find it.

### When to Use

Normally, a reference section is required for large or complex programs with many commands and operating procedures. Small programs tend to group related information closer together so any given subject is not hard to find, especially if the index is good. If this is true in your manual, then you may decide not to include a reference section.

### How to Write

See Chapter 8 for an in-depth look at how to write reference sections.

## Appendix

### Purpose

The appendix includes information about the software that is usually technical in nature and not often used. If it were included in the body of the manual, such information might serve only to confuse the user. The appendix is also used to cover highly technical topics of interest to only a few users but necessary to make the manual complete.

### Benefits

The appendix helps to reduce user confusion by eliminating highly technical information from the body of the manual and placing it out of the way but still available to those who are interested.

### When to Use

Use only if you have technical information that might confuse the user in the body of the manual. If the information will not confuse users, put it in the body of the manual where it will not go unread. Appendixes are often overlooked by users.

### How to Write

Each topic found in the appendix should have its own section. If there is more than one section, each should have an introduction explaining what is to follow and why it is important. Then discuss your subject in depth, using examples and illustrations where appropriate.

## Glossary

### Purpose

The glossary is used to define words that are unique to the program and computer-related words that may not be understood by some users.

### Benefits
The glossary aids those users who are not completely familiar with computers and reduces the chances of misinterpretation of instructions, which often results in user frustration.

### When to Use
A glossary should be included with all manuals. Even if your audience is experienced and you have avoided most technical terms, you may be using a word to which you give a slightly different meaning than does somebody else. It's better to have too many words in your glossary than too few.

### How to Write
List each word alphabetically, explaining as clearly as possible the definition of the word as it applies to the program. Try not to define a term with a word that is even more difficult. If you cannot avoid this, be sure to include that word in the glossary also.

## Index

### Purpose
The purpose of the index is to direct users to what they want to know about a program, even if they are not sure exactly how the subject is listed in the manual.

### Benefits
An index allows the user to find information about a program in a quick, convenient way. Not only will users appreciate the extra effort, but software reviewers will look kindly on you if you include one in your manual.

### When to Use
As a general rule of thumb, include an index in any manual with more than twenty pages.

### How to Write
Compiling an index can be both time consuming and tedious. The basic steps are the following:

1. Before you can begin, the manual must be complete and page numbers assigned.

2. Read the manual carefully, looking for main topics and subtopics. For example, "printing" could be considered a main topic and "inventory report" could be considered a subtopic of "printing." On the manuscript, underline the main topics with one color and subtopics with another color. Do this until you have completed the entire manual.

3. The next step is usually done with 3x5-inch index cards. Go back through the manual, and where you have underlined a major topic, put that topic on an index card by itself with the page number. When

you come across a subtopic, place the subject and page number on the relevant topic index card. Do this until you have finished the manual.

**4.** Editing the topics on the index cards is the next step. First sort them into alphabetical order (if you have not done so in the last step) and eliminate any duplication of entries by crossing them off the cards.

**5.** The last step is to put the cards into manuscript form so that they can be added to the manual. Using a typewriter or word processor, first list each main topic with relevant page numbers, then have the subtopics follow, sorted in alphabetical order (by word), with their relevant page numbers.

> Printing, 8, 21-28, 46, 67
> Balance Sheet, 22
> Income Statement, 24, 67
> Inventory Report, 25, 27
> Vendor List, 28, 46

## Quick Reference Card

### Purpose
From time to time, software users may forget a command or procedure, especially if it is not often used. The quick reference card is a summary of all the commands available, so that the user does not have to get the manual out and look up each command. It is usually printed on a heavy card stock and folded for ease of use.

### Benefits
Quick reference cards are a big time-saver and add to the professional appearance of the software package.

### When to Use
Although a quick reference card is not required for any software, it is a convenience that many software buyers expect and deserve. Include one if your budget permits.

### How to Write
Essentially, all you have to do is list all the commands used by the program along with what they do. If you have many commands, it is best to group the related commands together. (See Chapter 9 for an example of a quick reference card.)

Determining your manual's organization is the most crucial part of the entire manual planning stage. It lays the foundation on which you build the manual outline (discussed in the next chapter), and is the basis for the eventual writing of the manual. The more carefully you plan your manual, the easier you will find it to write an effective manual that meets the five aspects of manual organization: logic, sequence, relevance, balance, and consistency.

For complete examples of how each of these organizational elements can be used in practice, see the sample manual in Chapter 9 (Writing Your Manual).

**Lawford & Associates**

Before Jill completes the tentative manual plan, she must come up with a rough outline of the manual's organization. She knows that the organization of the manual must support the objectives set out for the manual.

Using the information she gathered about the audience and taking into consideration how she has decided to slant the manual to them, Jill decides to include the following organization elements in her manual. To show the relationship among the various sections of the manual and the way they support the manual's objectives, she puts together this chart.

**Organizational Element**

| | Easy-to-Use | Clearly Communicate | Sell Software |
|---|---|---|---|
| | **Manual Objectives** | | |
| Preface | | | ● |
| Table of Contents | ● | | |
| Introduction | | ● | |
| Getting Started | ● | | |
| Tutorial | ● | | |
| Reference Section | ● | | |
| Appendix | ● | | |
| Glossary | | ● | |
| Index | ● | | |
| Quick Reference Card | ● | | |

Each organizational element strongly supports at least one of the manual's objectives. She realizes that some sections also do carry into other objectives, but she has picked only the strongest objective each section supports to simplify the chart. Jill intends to show it to David to explain why she picked these particular elements to include in the manual.

With the rough organization of the manual complete, she is ready to complete the rest of the manual plan. Once the plan is approved by David, she can begin writing the detailed outline.

# 5. Outlining Your Manual

Tens of thousands of houses and office buildings are built each year in the United States. Each individual building consists of thousands of parts from hundreds of manufacturers. No two buildings are identical; even tract homes that appear the same on the outside have internal differences. One house may have a den where another has a bedroom. What all these buildings do have in common is that the builder had a plan in mind before starting, usually in the form of a blueprint.

Without a blueprint, a builder would have a tough time deciding what materials had to be ordered and then how to assemble the materials once they were delivered. An experienced builder would probably not have much difficulty erecting some sort of building, but most likely he would waste both time and materials as he would not be sure what the finished building would look like. If proper foresight is not taken, the house might end up unfit for use, not unlike many users manuals written today.

An outline for a software manual is as important to the manual writer as a blueprint is to a builder. An outline helps the writer to plan the manual and assemble the necessary "knowledge" and materials, and to manage the direction of the writing so that the completed manual is tailored to fit a particular audience. Like a blueprint, an outline does not specify everything that is to be included in a manual. Even blueprints leave the fine details up to the builder.

An outline is a planning tool—used by all writers for all types of writing—that gives the entire perspective of the manual before it is written, allowing the writer to check for the proper manual organization discussed in the previous chapter. Ensuring that all aspects of organization are included in the outline at this stage is much easier than waiting until the manual is written. It may help to think of the outline as a skeleton manual without all the details that clutter and obscure the essential framework of the manual.

Outlines not only help ensure well-organized manuals, they also help prevent writer's block. From time to time, most writers experience a period when they cannot seem to write. Often, this block is a result of not knowing what to write. An outline specifies, step by step, what the writer is to write. Furthermore, an outline gives an indication of where to start writing. You do not write a manual by starting from the beginning and finishing at the end. The parts are written at different times and later fitted into the whole. The outline both establishes the whole of the manual and suggests a place to start and place to stop.

**Before You Outline: Preliminary Research**

## The Ever-Important Audience

In Chapter 3 you were urged to find out who the audience is for your manual before you begin writing, and many possibilities were outlined. This point cannot be stressed too much, as the audience significantly affects the course of outlining. If you think you are at the outlining stage and have not yet seriously considered the manual's audience, stop where you are and do so. Once you have thoroughly and exhaustively examined your audience, make a list of their characteristics and indicate how you intend to slant the writing to them. Tape it on the wall in front of your desk; it will help you to keep in mind at all times who you are writing for. If you have to, read it every day, or several times each day, whatever it takes to drill the audience into your mind so that they are reflected in the outlining and later in the writing stages of the manual.

## Know the Software

Get to know the workings, operation, and idiosyncrasies of the software you are writing the manual for. You cannot expect to create a complete outline unless you know the software completely.

If you are able to start your planning when the software itself is being planned, all the better. If you do not start the manual until the program is complete or almost complete, start by examining the programmer's notes and documentation. Talk to the programmer and find out everything you can about the program. Before you begin interrogating the programmer, plan your questions. Conduct the interview as though you were investigating a government cover-up for the *Washington Post*. Find out the good and bad features of the program and why they are good and bad.

Once you have gotten all the information you can from the programmer, start using the program yourself. Spend days, weeks if necessary, using the program in every possible way, leaving no possibility unexamined. For example, a database program may be easy to set up for a mailing list, but if set up for an inventory system, it may be extremely complicated. You need to know how to handle all situations. Practicing with the program will bring up more questions to ask the programmer. Ask them, leaving no questions unanswered.

Take abundant notes, keeping them sorted into appropriate categories for later use. Your practice with the program should suggest what should be included in the manual and how to approach certain topics and should help you devise practical and realistic examples and exercises.

Don't think that most of the audience will not be interested in the advanced features of the program. You can't skimp on explaining those features. It's your job to write a comprehensive manual, not make judgments on how the program will be used. Be thorough. The more exhaustive your study of the program, the better and more useful your manual will be.

**Drafting the Outline**

Once you know your audience and the software as a mother knows her children, you are ready to begin outlining your manual. The easiest way to proceed is to use a word processor, which will allow you to make corrections, change and insert and delete text at random, availing itself readily to outline creation. (See "For More Information" in Chapter 9 for recommendations on word processing software.) A second, but inferior, choice is to use 5x8-inch lined index cards, using a separate card for each major topic, with minor topics listed below on each card. (See Figure 5-1.) While this allows you to rearrange and insert cards into the outline, the process is awkward and much slower than using a word processor.

**Figure 5-1**
**Using Index Cards**
**For Manual Outlining**
*This is a sample of one of the index cards used to outline the Preface of the fictional software, Electronic Encyclopedia. You have to devise your own system for outlining that best meets your needs.*

---

**Front of Index Card**

**Preface**

1. Welcome the user
2. State the purpose of the program
   a) Computer-based electronic encyclopedia
   b) Allows users to look up articles on thousands of subjects
3. Who is the intended audience?
   a) Every computer owner who needs the speed and convenience of computerized information retrieval

---

**Back of Index Card**

4. Features of Electronic Encyclopedia
   a) Retrieve articles on over 10,000 different subjects; each article ranges in length from 200 to 5,000 words
   b) Search for subjects using any combination of search words user wants
   c) Compile research into one report
   d) Print portions or complete articles for later use
5. Benefits of program for users
   a) Fast retrieval of information reduces time spent researching
   b) User receives updates of the articles every six months, giving the user always current information

Once you have decided on how you will go about writing your outline, follow these guidelines during the actual outlining process.

**1.** If you have not already done so, decide on which sections of the manual you intend to include, such as "getting started," "tutorial," "reference section," and so on. These sections of the manual are your largest divisions and provide the basic building blocks of the manual.

**2.** Devise a filing system (perhaps one manila filing folder for each section) so that you can file your research under the appropriate section. This system will reduce the amount of time you spend later searching for important information.

**3.** Once you have separated your notes into the proper sections, begin going through each section of notes, using the information to break down the section into major headings such as the introduction of the section, major features, and summary. Different software will require different major headings. Follow the principles of organization you learned in the last chapter.

**4.** Once the major headings have been established, the next step is to further divide the section into minor headings, separating the major headings into digestible bits of information. Include all necessary detailed information along with examples, exercises, and illustrations. In the outline you do not have to specify the exact examples, exercises, or illustrations, but at the very least indicate where and how many of them you will include under each minor section. As you create the outline, you will find that you want to change, insert, and delete items. At first the outline will have little form, but as you continue, it will begin to take shape. Outlining may take several days, or even weeks, depending on the complexity of the program. The more complete you can make the outline, the easier the manual will be to write later.

**5.** After the first draft of the outline is complete, you should have a good feeling for how the finished manual will look. Before you begin writing the manual, however, take the time to review and edit the outline. Don't do this immediately after you finish the first draft; take a break for a couple of days and do something else. This extra time helps to make you more objective about the outline. When you go back to rewrite it, you will do it from a fresher viewpoint. Look at it with a careful eye to organization, looking for weakness in structure. The time to correct organizational problems is before you begin to write the manual. Also get the programmer and others to look the outline over; they may be able to find problems that you cannot see. Make any necessary changes and corrections based on this review.

Your manual outline is now complete and will serve as your guide to writing the manual. While it does not specify the exact way you will write the manual, it does provide a framework which you know is a sound structure. The following section shows the outline Jill Bates wrote for the manual for Home Mortgage Calculator.

After Jill's manual plan was approved by David during the Monday meeting, she had to wait several weeks while the program was being written before she could begin the outlining of the manual. Each Monday she would stop by Lawford & Associates to check on the program's progress and talk with David. Usually, she would get to see parts of the program running and thus gain a better perspective of how the final program would operate.

After three weeks the preliminary version of Home Mortgage Calculator is complete and David gives Jill a preliminary copy of Home Mortgage Calculator for her to work with at home on the IBM personal computer she has already borrowed.

After spending much time becoming intimately familiar with the program, Jill becomes confident she can start outlining the manual. During the week she writes an outline with her word processor, completing it for David's approval during their next Monday meeting.

At the meeting on Monday, Jill shows David the outline and gets his comments on it. He gives her the go-ahead to start writing a preliminary version of the manual to be used during the beta-testing of the software.

Jill's outline for the manual, incorporating David's suggestions, is this:

    I. Title Page
      A. Program title
      B. Publisher name
   II. Copyright Page
      A. Customer service information
      B. Copyright notice
      C. Publisher name and address
      D. Author credits
      E. Acknowledgments
  III. Preface
      A. Welcome
      B. Program features
      C. Program benefits
      D. Equipment requirements
      E. Manual overview
  IV. Table of Contents
   V. Introduction
      A. Overview of section
      B. How to use manual
        1. Getting started
        2. Tutorial
        3. Reference section
        4. Appendix
        5. Glossary & Index
        6. Quick reference card
      C. How to follow manual examples

          1. Entering commands

          2. Recognizing computer responses

    D. Terminology

    E. Overview of program

          1. Why use the program

          2. The calculator screen

          3. The calculator window

          4. Experimenting with financing terms

          5. The comparison window

    F. Program control

    G. Error messages

          1. Program errors

          2. Computer errors

    H. Section summary

VI. Getting Started

    A. What you need to get started

          1. Hardware requirements

          2. Diskette requirements

          3. Optional equipment

    B. Preparing the working copy

          1. Why preparation is necessary

          2. Steps for making the working copy

    C. Printer setup

          1. Steps for preparing the working copy for printer

VII. Tutorial

    A. Introduction to tutorial

    B. Loading the program

          1. How to load when computer is off; listed steps

          2. How to load when computer is on; listed steps

          3. Need illustrations of title screen and calculator screen of program for these steps

          4. Summary of how to load the program

    C. Using the calculator screen

          1. Overview of subsection

          2. The calculator screen (need illustration of screen)

          3. The cursor

          4. Moving the cursor with the tab key (example)

          5. Moving the cursor with the shift and tab keys (example)

          6. Entering data into the calculator window (example)

          7. How to correct data entry errors

             a. Method 1 (example)

             b. Method 2 (example)

          8. Making your first calculation

             a. Example 1 (steps and illustration)

             b. Example 2 (steps)

             c. Example 3 (steps)

          9. More practice

             a. Exercise 1

      b. Exercise 2

      c. Exercise 3

      d. Exercise 4

    10. Printing the calculator screen (example; steps)

    11. Summary of subsection

  D. Displaying and printing comparison tables

    1. Overview of subsection

    2. Displaying your first table

      a. Example 1 (steps and illustrations)

      b. Example 2 (steps and illustrations)

    3. Making different comparisons

    4. More practice

    5. Printing tables (steps)

    6. Summary of subsection

  E. Exiting the program

    1. Steps

    2. Summary of subsection

VIII. Reference Section

  A. Introduction to section

  B. How to use the reference section

  C. Loading program

  1. Purpose

  2. Computer is off

  3. Computer is on

  D. Using the calculator screen

    1. Purpose

    2. How to solve for:

      a. Purchase price

      b. Percentage down payment

      c. Loan term

      d. Annual interest rate

      e. Monthly payment

  E. Displaying and printing comparison tables

    1. Purpose

    2. How to display and print:

      a. Table 1

      b. Table 2

  F. Exiting the program

    1. Purpose

    2. Explanation

IX. Appendices

  A. Appendix A: Error messages

  B. Appendix B: How Home Mortgage Calculator makes its calculations [to be provided by David]

  C. Appendix C: Technical notes [to be provided by David]

X. Glossary

XI. Index

# 6. Writing Style

Writing style is how you write, the unique way you select words to communicate with the reader. Some writers write lean, terse prose, while others have a rich, flowing style. Good style can make the reader see or feel what the writer wants him to; poor style can fail to give the reader the proper image.

There is no best style. You cannot hope to imitate the comprehensible, learned writing of Isaac Asimov or the imagination and excitement of Carl Sagan's writing. You must be yourself. Write to inform, to instruct, to communicate. Keep your audience in mind at all times. Try to write as if you were the reader and you could dictate to the author how you want to proceed. Don't worry about style; rather, worry about getting your message across to the reader.

There are no hard and fast rules about writing style, but good writing is always clear, coherent, and concise. Your manual must reflect these attributes; otherwise you fail your readers. They rightly expect to be informed and instructed about the software they purchase. Your writing does not have to read like poetry, but it must tell the user how to use the program. If you can make the instructions interesting, you have begun to develop your own style.

This book cannot hope to teach you all about writing. There are already many books devoted to that challenge. However, it will point out ten areas where manual writers often have problems. After you read each guideline, take the time to think about how it might affect your writing. After you have thought each one over, make a promise to yourself to practice what you have learned. Only through practice will you develop a style that keeps the users interested while it informs them about the intricacies of their software purchase.

## Establishing a Point

Before you began a footrace through a forest, you would want a map that showed your location, your destination, and the shortest path between the two. The same goes for the user of your manual. If he does not know where you are leading him, he may not recognize where he is once you have brought him there. Therefore, you must establish the point you are making early in the mind of the user, giving broad concepts before you plunge into the many details that explain them. Preparing the user for what to expect provides the foundation he needs to thoroughly understand what follows. This is especially important in writing manuals because they often introduce a new subject to the user. Their instructional nature demands that the user be gently introduced to topics before all the particulars are covered.

The most practical places to establish a point are in the introductory section of a manual, the introductory paragraph of a section, and the topic sentence at the beginning of a paragraph. We have already discussed organization on the manual and sectional level, so let's examine how it applies to the paragraph.

Compare the following passages.

1. After you turn the printer on, turn the printer off-line. Be sure you have paper in the printer. Now press the form feed button once. If you hold it down too long you might get multiple form feeds, wasting both your time and paper.

2. The easiest way to advance the paper in your printer—one sheet at a time—is to use the form feed button. Before you try this, check to see if the paper is properly loaded in the printer. Once the paper is adjusted, put your printer off-line by pressing the off-line button found on top of the printer. The form feed option will not work if your printer is on-line. Now press the form feed button once. It is located next to the off-line button on top of the printer. Be careful not to hold the button down too long or you might get multiple form feeds, causing you to waste several sheets of paper.

The first paragraph jumps right in and the user is not sure where it is going. There is no topic sentence to indicate what is being discussed. It is only when the paragraph is completely read that you get an indication of its purpose.

The second paragraph introduces its subject with a topic sentence. The user knows immediately what will be covered in the paragraph and is prepared for the details that follow.

Try to write your paragraphs (and all that you write) so that they establish your point quickly for the user.

**Choosing the Right Words**

Which sentence is better:

The sticker is fixed upon the printing device.

The serial number sticker is found on the rear back panel of the Epson MX-80.

Both of the above sentences could mean the same thing. Again, however, the first sentence is so ambiguous that it could mean a variety of things. The second sentence is not open to interpretation: you know what kind of sticker is being referred to, where it is, and on what printer.

Strunk and White, in their book *The Elements of Style*, claim that "the surest way to arouse and hold the attention of the user is by being specific, definite, and concrete" in writing. This approach is doubly important to the manual writer. More often than not, the subject of manuals is dry and uninspiring. Not only that, but accuracy is important so that the user will not inadvertently make time-consuming mistakes. Choosing the right word for the right occasion breathes life into dry instruction and leaves no room for misinterpretation.

To aid in your search for the right words, here are some guidelines.

*Favor short words over long.* Not only are short words more easily understood by users, they are often more bold and direct.

| Avoid | Substitute |
|---|---|
| component | part |
| facilitate | help, make easier |
| implement | do, use |
| terminate | end, exit |
| utilize | use |
| initialize | start, begin |

*Favor concrete words over abstract.* Concrete words produce more vivid images and reduce misinterpretation by the user.

| Avoid | Substitute |
|---|---|
| input (noun) | numbers, text, data |
| large amount | 500,789 |
| memory | read only memory, user memory |
| output (noun) | screen, report |
| peripheral | printer, modem |
| several | three, four |

*Favor simple words over fancy.* Simple words are more understandable to a larger number of users and help make your writing more informal and conversational.

| Avoid | Substitute |
|---|---|
| peruse | read |
| purge | erase |
| queue | list |
| rapidity | speed |
| replicate | copy |

*Favor everyday words over jargon.* Jargon (or slang) terms are words peculiar to a specific profession, such as computers or accounting, that have little or no meaning to people outside the field. Jargon should not be confused with the indispensable technical terms or nomenclature used in the various professions.

| Avoid | Substitute |
|---|---|
| bug | error |
| bombed | failed, stopped |
| crashed | failed, stopped |
| hacker | programmer |
| kill | stop, end |
| power down | turn off |

*Favor words over symbols, initials, and abbreviations.* Words are easier to read than symbols, initials, or abbreviations and prevent any possible misinterpretation of meaning. If you elect to use the latter, be sure you define them the first time they are used.

| Avoid | Substitute |
|---|---|
| % | percent |
| CPU | central processing unit |
| e.g. | for example |
| etc. | and so on, and so forth |
| hex | hexadecimal |
| lpm | lines per minute |
| RAM | random access memory |

*Avoid clichés and overused language.* Clichés and overused words are threadbare and lack force.

| Avoid | Substitute |
|---|---|
| impact | affect, have an effect |
| interface | work together, connection |
| minimize | lower, reduce, decrease |

**Eliminate**
acid test
each and every
stands to reason

**Avoiding Wordiness**

Having extra words in a sentence, or extra sentences in a paragraph, is like wearing a pair of glasses you don't need—both blur what is ahead. Consider the following sentences:

Many of the writers of manuals, overall, hopefully attempt to do a very good job

Many manual writers try to do a good job.

Not only is the first sentence incoherent, it has six more words than the second while trying to say the same thing. Wordiness is an opponent of both conciseness and clarity. Say what you have to say with the least number of words. However, don't skimp on words if they are necessary to make your point clear. Other examples are:

| Avoid | Substitute |
|---|---|
| have a tendency to | tend to |
| in terms of programming | programming |
| many of the plotters | many plotters |
| the field of data processing | data processing |
| the number of entries | entries |
| there are some errors | some errors will |
| that will | |

| Eliminate | |
|---|---|
| any | both |
| certain | eminent |
| hopefully | in fact |
| in general | in particular |
| overall | really |

**Pace**

The pace of your writing has to do with how quickly you reveal information to the user. The more information you pack into sentences, the faster the pace; the less information you pack in the same number of sentences, the slower the pace.

You must adjust the pace of your writing to fit the situation. New or difficult material should be presented slowly. It should give the user time to digest each point as it is presented. In contrast, if what you are writing is summary or is familiar to the user, you can pick up the pace; otherwise your writing might drag down and you might lose the reader's interest. As you write you manual, you must decide what material should be fast-paced and which should be slow-paced. For example:

1. To print the income statement report, you must first go to the main menu and select the report menu, then enter the income statement report option. After each option enter the appropriate format options along with the number of copies you want printed and today's date.

2. Printing the income statement report takes several steps. First, you must start from the main menu and select the report menu option. After the report menu appears on your screen, you must select the income statement option. This brings you to the point where you can begin entering the report's formatting options, the number of copies to be printed, and today's date.

The pace of the first paragraph would be too fast if you were introducing the subject of printing an income statement report for the first time. If you were only summarizing the subject, however, the pace might be appropriate.

The slower pace of the second paragraph is more suitable for presenting the information for the first time to the user. Each significant fact has a sentence all to its own, giving the user time to let the material sink in before something new is discussed.

Besides varying the length of sentences, you can also affect the pace by means of paragraph length, headings, and illustrations. Short paragraphs provide a brief resting place each time they end, giving the user time to absorb the material. Long paragraphs do not provide such "rest areas" and so increase the writing pace. Headings and illustrations also interrupt reading and give additional time for material to sink in.

## Examples and Comparisons

One way to make your prose more lively and clearer is to use examples and comparisons. An *example* illustrates a point; a *comparison* contrasts it with something else.

Examples are easy to write and are most appropriate for instructional material. In this chapter there have been many words, sentences, and paragraphs given to illustrate style guidelines. You should include examples in your manual writing. Not only do they clarify what you want to say, they make your prose livelier and more interesting.

There are three kinds of comparisons you can make: similes, metaphors, and analogies. *Similes* are explicit comparisons that always contain the word *as* or *like* in them.

Inserting a floppy diskette into a disk drive is like putting a slice of bread in a toaster.

With a *metaphor*, on the other hand, a comparison is implied, not stated explicitly.

The new computer program, INSIGHT, is more intelligent than most college professors.

*Analogies*, like similes and metaphors make a comparison, but with an added dimension. Analogies compare things that are not from the same general classification. For example, the way a computer program works is compared to the way the human mind works. This device is especially useful in that it clarifies something new to the user by likening it to something that is familiar. In most cases, analogies run a paragraph or more in length. For example:

The master detective Sherlock Holmes is known for always getting the bad guy. As with most fictional detectives, his creator, Sir Arthur Conan Doyle, gave Sherlock a particular way to solve the crimes he was hired to solve.

After a crime was committed, Sherlock would go to the scene of the crime and look for clues. After examining the evidence carefully, and perhaps doing some additional legwork, he would solve the crime by making sense out of the information he collected. Sherlock is well known for his ability in deductive reasoning.

The recently developed software package INSIGHT uses deductive reasoning much like Sherlock Holmes did in his many adventures. INSIGHT allows you to enter random bits of information and then it determines what, if any, relationship exists among the data you entered. Not unlike the solutions of Sherlock Holmes, the results IN-SIGHT provides can be simply amazing.

The easiest way to get into trouble making comparisons is by not being logically consistent. You will confuse rather than clarify your writing. For example, comparing the spin of a floppy diskette in a disk drive to the spin of a merry-go-round makes little sense, but comparing it to the spin of a record on a turntable is sensible. A merry-go-round does spin like a floppy diskette in a disk drive, but it is an amusement park machine that is designed to be ridden by passengers. A record spinning on a turntable, on the other hand, is designed to transfer information stored on the record—usually music—to the record player's amplifier. As a spinning floppy diskette also is designed to transfer information from it to another device—the computer's memory—the comparison is closer to the spinning record example than the merry-go-round example, which does not transfer any information.

**Tone**

Tone is the manner in which you express your words: formal or informal, unfeeling or emotional, unpretentious or condescending. Instructional writing should try to imitate the tone of oral instruction, as that is what most users are accustomed to following. This means that the tone you want to get across is informal, friendly, and even sympathetic. If you do this, the user will come to trust you.

Besides following the guidelines suggested in this chapter, one of the best ways to create this tone is to write in the second person, using *you* and *your* throughout the manual. Compare the following passages and decide which one you would prefer to read in a software manual.

1. After the user completes the backup procedure, he should store the diskette in a safe location. If the user does not heed this advice, the diskette may become damaged and the information stored on it lost forever.

2. After you complete the backup procedure, be sure to store the diskette in a safe place. Otherwise, the information on the diskette might be lost.

The first passage is cold and unfriendly. The second sounds like it might have been said by your mother.

Remember most of all to use tone to make your prose inviting to read, but don't let it get in the way of clarity.

**Voice**

Which of these sentences sounds more forceful:

The working copy is to be inserted in disk drive A.

Insert the working copy in disk drive A.

Both sentences say the same thing, but the second is more direct and forceful and uses fewer words. It has a sense of urgency and sounds like an oral command. The first sentence is clear and correct, but it lacks the vitality of the second.

The second sentence is written in the active voice. The first sentence, in contrast, is written in the passive voice.

You should use the active voice in your manuals, especially in the tutorial sections. Like tone, the active voice makes your writing come alive by making it sound like oral instructions. It is friendly and to the point. Would you tell a friend *the computer is to be turned on?* Never. You would tell your friend to *turn on the computer.*

This is not to say that the passive voice should never be used. If the object of the action is more important than the subject, or if the active voice is awkward, or if you want a sentence to stand out in the middle of a group of active voice sentences, use the passive voice. Nevertheless, you should develop the habit of writing in the active voice. It is almost always preferred.

**Tense**

Write in the present tense. Doing so implies that action is occurring now and it complements the active voice and friendly tone of your writing. Which sentence sounds better:

> After you choose option six, the mailing list menu was displayed.

> As you chose option six, the mailing list menu is displayed.

> When option six is chosen, the mailing list menu will be displayed.

The first sentence, written in the past tense, sounds awkward even though it is grammatically correct. The last sentence, written in the future tense, is grammatically correct but it lacks the immediacy of "now" for an action that occurs immediately. The second sentence, written in the present tense, has a sense of simplicity and immediacy. This use of tense corresponds with your goal of making your writing sound as if it were coming from a friend.

Be consistent when you write in the present tense. Do not shift tenses; you will confuse the user.

**Consistency**

One of the easiest ways to confuse your readers is to be inconsistent in your use of words or phrases, numbers, symbols, spelling, capital letters, punctuation, and abbreviations.

> Don't use the phrase *video display terminal* in one place and *monitor* in another. Decide what phrase you want to call something and use it throughout the manual.

> Don't spell out the number *five* in one place and then use the numeral 5 in another.

> Don't use the symbol % in one place and then use the word *percent* in another.

> Don't spell the word *disk* in one place and then spell the word *disc* in another.

Don't capitalize all letters of *ENTER* in one place and then capitalize only the first letter of *Enter* in another.

Don't punctuate a series with one comma, as in *one, two and three,* in one place and then punctuate a series with two commas, as in *one, two, and three,* in another.

Don't abbreviate the phrase "disk operating system" *(DOS)* in one place and then use the phrase by itself in another.

To prevent such inconsistencies from occurring, you should develop your own style sheet. You either can create one before you begin writing the manual, or you can create it as you go along. If you have trouble determining what style you want to use, use one of the style guides listed at the end of this chapter. When your manual is complete, you'll want to go back and make sure that everything in it conforms to the style sheet. This is best done during the proofreading stage, discussed in Chapter 9.

## Grammar and Punctuation

The area of grammar and punctuation, like writing style, is an inexact science. There are sets of rules for both that you probably learned in school and this book will not cover them. What is important about them is that they are used to enhance the clarity of your writing. Improper grammar and punctuation can make your writing ambiguous and might mislead the user.

## Reading Your Writing Out Loud

The best way to prevent any stylistic or wording errors in your writing is to perform this simple test: read your writing out loud, and if it sounds correct, then it probably is correct. You might want to go so far as to read the manual to a friend, getting his reaction. This principle relates to making your writing sound like a friend talking. You can apply it to the first draft, to later drafts, and even during the proofreading stage. If you doubt whether a sentence or paragraph is correct or not, then, read it out loud in context. You'll be surprised how often this method works.

## Lawford & Associates

Before Jill begins writing the first draft of the manual, she decides to develop her own style sheet to ensure consistency throughout her manual.

To keep it as simple as possible, she gets several sheets of blank paper and at the top of each one writes the name of a stylistic factor. Under each topic she makes notes about how she intends to deal with particular situations. She leaves plenty of room on each sheet to add additional notes as she proceeds with the actual writing of the manual and runs into additional style situations.

Whenever she comes up against any style questions she cannot answer on her own, she looks up the subject in one of the many style manuals she has collected over the years. So that she does not lose track of her style sheet, Jill places all the sheets of paper in a file folder labeled "Home Mortgage Calculator Style Manual" and puts it next to her computer.

Here is an abbreviated version of Jill's style manual. Notice how informal and personalized it is.

### Abbreviations
Use as few abbreviations as possible. Use only those that are industry standards such as DOS or K. Even when using common abbreviations, always spell them out the first time they are used in the main body of the manual.

Never abbreviate "Home Mortgage Calculator" or "video display terminal," even though they are often used in the manual.

### Capitalization
Always capitalize "Home Mortgage Calculator" and "Lawford & Associates."

Capitalize all words in subheads except articles, conjunctions, and prepositions.

### Jargon & Terminology
Use "video display terminal," not: CRT, VDT, terminal, or monitor.
Use "diskette" or "floppy diskette," not: disk or disc.

### Numbers
Spell out numbers 0 through 10 and write out numbers greater than 10.

Write out numbers when used as figure designations, such as Figure 1.

### Other
Always use the ampersand in Lawford & Associates.

### Punctuation
In a series separated by commas, always include a comma before the "and."

### Spelling
Don't misspell: appendix, experience, summary.

**For More Information** There is a flood of good books on composition and writing style. You would be wise to have most of the ones listed below on your desk when you are writing.

*The Elements of Technical Writing* (Harcourt Brace Jovanovich, 1980), by Joseph A. Alvarez, is a storehouse of important information for the manual writer. Not only does he cover the basics of technical writing, he discusses, in depth, writing style, punctuation, and grammar. It is excellent for reference.

Two books devoted exclusively to writing style are *The Elements of Style* (Macmillan, 1972), by William Strunk, Jr. and E. B. White, and *Edit Yourself* (W.W. Norton & Co., 1982), by Bruce Ross-Larson. Strunk and White's book takes a little more than an hour to read and offers random tidbits about improving your writing style. Ross-Larson's book lists thousands of words and phrases that you should try to avoid and gives suggestions for substitutes. It is a book to be referred to rather than read.

Two highly recommended guides that can be used to help you create your own style sheet are *Manual of Style* (University of Chicago Press, Thirteenth Edition, 1982) and the *Government Printing Office Style Manual* (U.S. Government Printing Office, 1973). Both offer suggestions for spelling, capitalization, abbreviation, and so on.

If you have difficulty choosing the best word, you need to buy a good thesaurus and dictionary. *The Doubleday Roget's Thesaurus* (Doubleday, 1977) is arranged like a dictionary and is easy to use. Almost any dictionary will aid you in spelling and in obtaining the exact meaning of a word.

*If you write with a word processor,* you should look into one of the writing analysis programs. GRAMMATIK, by Wang Electronic Publishing, works with many different computers and will find poor style that you missed. It looks for overused, redundant, and trite phrases, among many other things.

# 7. How to Write Tutorials

Teaching algebra to a high school student is a difficult task. The teacher must first assess the student's math background and then lead the student from there step by step through the procedure to solve equations. This process involves several teaching techniques, including reading assignments, class lectures with illustrative examples, individual assistance, and homework assignments to practice the material. After much practice, the student should have learned the techniques of algebra and be able to apply them on his own.

Teaching a user to operate a program is similar to teaching a student algebra, except that all the teaching must be accomplished with a manual. Unlike the classroom teacher, you don't have the opportunity to answer individual questions or provide individual help. You must, however, assess the user's background in the software application. Because you can't talk with each user before he begins reading the manual, you have to make some assumptions based on the perceived audience. From there you must lead the user step by step through the use of the program on the computer. Since you cannot be a private tutor, a tutorial approach to teaching is the next best approach.

A tutorial is a cookbook, hand-holding, step-by-step method of teaching the concepts and techniques of using a program. It should bring the user from a state of incomplete or nonexistent knowledge about the program to a state of complete understanding of its operation and use. This chapter is devoted to showing you how you can write tutorials that successfully teach a user how to operate a program.

## When to Use Tutorials

Like most sections of a user manual, the tutorial is not mandatory. Its use depends on the type of program and the audience. You should include a tutorial in your manual if any of the following are true:

- If the manual is to provide the user's first introduction to the program. If the user already knows how to use the program or is taught the program operation in some other way, such as in a classroom, a reference approach may be more appropriate.
- If the program is complex or involves many steps. Utilities or games often don't need tutorials because of their relatively simple operation.

• If the user is apt to be a novice about either computers or the program application. The less experienced the user, the more hand-holding he requires.

## The Novice vs. Expert Dilemma

How do you write a tutorial so that it doesn't expect too much of the beginner and at the same time doesn't waste the expert's time with needless detail? This is a common problem, because most programs are used by beginners and experts alike. There are no easy solutions. As has been repeated over and over in this book, the way you choose to deal with this dilemma depends on the software and audience—there is no one best answer. To help you decide on the best approach, here are some suggestions along with their advantages and disadvantages.

• Try writing two different manuals, one for beginners and another for experts. The introductory manual can be tailored specifically for beginners needs, covering all the basics. The expert manual can cover the same material at a faster pace and can include more advanced applications. When the novice has gone through the first manual and feels confident with it, he can go to the expert manual if he has a need for the advanced applications.

While this may be the ideal way out of the dilemma, it is expensive in terms of time and printing costs. Both manuals would have to be included with each software package. On the other hand, the cost of manuals is often insignificant in relation to the retail price of a program. The extra costs will affect mostly inexpensive programs such as games or home programs.

• Within the same manual have two different tutorials—one for beginners and one for advanced users—and leave the rest of the manual the same. As with the previous method, both the beginner and expert have tutorials tailored to their own needs. The other sections would have to be written for the beginner and might cause some wasted effort for the expert, but much less than if the whole manual were written on that level.

The cost of this alternative is also high in time and printing, but less so than having two distinct manuals. As a compromise, this may be one of the best routes to take to solve the dilemma.

• Write only one tutorial, but section off parts specifically designed for beginners and experts. While this does separate the information, it can be confusing for the reader. Novices will probably want to read the advanced material anyway and may be confused by it. Experts will have to waste time turning pages, looking for headings telling them what to read and what not to read. This might be the best approach when the advanced material is not great in proportion to the entire tutorial; it can be sectioned off at the end of the tutorial, separated from the main, beginner material.

• A variation of the above might be to have one tutorial but put advanced or technical information in an appendix. This is perhaps not as effective since the expert will have to wade through a lot of beginner material, but at least the advanced material is included and available. This may be a good choice when the program is unique and many experts may not be familiar with it.

• You might tailor the tutorial to novices and tailor the reference section of the manual for experts. The novice would use the tutorial to learn the program and, after gaining experience, use the reference section for advanced learning. The expert, if he wants, can ignore the tutorial and read the reference section to learn the basics. Some reference sections assume you have read the tutorial and don't cover everything, so you must write the reference section assuming the reader has not read the tutorial.

• Ignore the dilemma and tailor the manual for novices. You may end up irritating expert users, but if they will be in the minority of users, this may be the most logical option.

## Guidelines for Writing Tutorials

Listed below are some general guidelines that apply whenever you write tutorials. Read them and then keep them in mind as you read about the steps you must take to write a tutorial, presented in the next section.

1. As with all the writing in your manual, slant the tutorial, its examples and exercises, and so on, to fit the needs of the audience and application. Terminology and exercises designed for certified public accountants are not appropriate if all the users are accounting clerks.

2. Present only one idea, point, concept, or technique at a time. Don't overwhelm the user by giving too much information at once. People learn more easily, and remember longer, when information is presented in small, easily understandable segments.

3. Not all tutorials have to be long. Adjust their length to fit the needs of the user and the complexity of the program.

4. If a program is complex, you might want to divide the tutorial into sections and then break each section down into segments that present one piece of information at a time. As a rule of thumb, each section should take no more than thirty minutes to complete. If it does, divide the tutorial into smaller sections. For example, a simple home program might have the tutorial in one section because the user can complete it in less than thirty minutes, but an integrated accounting package with general ledger, accounts receivable, and accounts payable might be first divided into logical sections, then further divided into logical subsections, each taking about thirty minutes to complete.

5. Whether you have only one tutorial section or many, always group related ideas, points, concepts, and techniques together, both on the section and segment level. For example, daily start-up procedures for an accounting program should be discussed all at one time, not separated in two or more different sections.

6. Arrange sections and segments so that they follow a logical sequence. You might arrange the tutorial in chronological order, or

you might begin the tutorial with the most crucial procedures, then cover the less essential ones. The nature of the software application determines the logical sequence.

**7.** Use illustrations throughout the tutorial. It is especially important to show the user what the screens or printed reports should look like. As will be discussed in Chapter 10 (Illustrating Your Manual), illustrations greatly add to the understanding of new material and make the manual more interesting to read.

**8.** As will be explained in this chapter, each tutorial segment is broken down into five parts. It is important to use graphic design devices, such as headings or boxes, to separate reading material and hands-on material. The user must easily recognize when it is time to do an example or exercise on the computer. Examples of this point are shown later in this chapter.

**9.** All examples and exercises must be realistic, relevant, and practical. Anything else is distracting and does not contribute to the learning process. Finding and writing good ones is hard work and must take the audience into consideration. You may even have to test your examples and exercises on users to see if they meet this criterion.

**10.** All material, examples, exercises, and illustrations must be 100 percent accurate. Mistakes of any kind will confuse the reader and reduce the teaching ability of your tutorial. They also give a bad impression of the software, even though it is the manual that is at fault. Go to extreme lengths to ensure all information is correct.

## Writing the Tutorial Segments

The basic segments of a tutorial are its foundation. The segments are grouped together to make sections, and the various sections (if more than one are needed) add up to the total tutorial. As the segments are the most important, they are what we will emphasize here. Here are guidelines for writing tutorial segments. Refer to figure 7-1 for an example.

**1.** Each segment starts with an introduction that explains what is covered in the segment, why it is important, and when to use it. If this segment is related to previous segments, you should show how they interrelate. For example, in Figure 7-1 you see a tutorial segment from the fictitious program Electronic Encyclopedia. The segment opens by explaining what the segment is about (one-word searches), explains why this is important (you must understand one-word searches before you can learn about search phrases), and describes when this is to be used (most of the time). The interrelationship of this segment with others is implied in the statement that this segment must be understood before more advanced searches are covered.

**2.** Describe the steps necessary to perform the action being described, if doing so is applicable to the information being explained. These are not detailed steps, but a general overview of the procedure. This overview only introduces the procedure to the user

Writing Software User Manuals

for the first time. Leave the details for the next step. In our example, a new heading begins the portion of this segment that gives a general overview of the procedure being taught.

3. Now that the user understands what the procedure is all about and how to perform it, walk the user through an actual example of the procedure. This is hands-on practice, so you should use some graphic device, such as a heading or box, to let the user know that this example is to be tried on the computer. Then, step by step, carefully instruct the user what he has to do to perform the sample procedure, key by key. Don't leave any room for misinterpretation. Use illustrations to show what the screen looks like, or what reports look like. Be sure to include the correct answer so that the user can check his progress. If necessary, explain to the reader how to correct mistakes if they arise, such as keying in the wrong data. The number of examples will depend on the complexity of the segment being taught.

In our example, this section is blocked off by a box to call attention to it. Then the actual procedure is detailed, and illustrations of the screen show the user exactly what is going on.

4. Now that the user has practical experience, it's a good idea to give practical exercises for additional practice and reinforcement of the newly learned skill. Unlike the above example, exercises do not hand-hold the user through the steps, but only provide the raw data to practice with and the results to check the user's progress. Not all segments require additional exercises; this again depends on your audience and the segment being taught.

In our example, there are five exercises given for additional practice. As with the example, the exercises have been boxed separately to let the user know that the exercises are different from the example. Even though the example here does not show the results of the exercises, you should always include them in your manual.

5. This last step is to summarize what was just learned. In most cases, this summary does not have to be extensive; only the highlights should be reiterated. Using a graphic device like bullets is useful to direct the attention of the user to each point. A summary helps reinforce the learning. If, after reading the summary, the user notices that some point of the summary is not clear, he can take the time now to find out what he still doesn't understand before continuing.

In our example the main points learned in the segment are listed and bullets are used to bring attention to them.

**Figure 7-1
Sample Tutorial Segment
Electronic Encyclopedia**

**Conducting a One-Word Search**

Before we get into more complex features of Electronic Encyclope-dia, let's find out how you can conduct simple searches for the infor-mation you need, using only one search word. Once you understand this basic operating procedure, you should have no problem con-ducting more complex searches, using search phrases. You can use the one-word search for almost all your needs and may come to find out that you use this feature of Electronic Encyclopedia more than any other.

**How to Conduct a One-Word Search** Let's say that you want to search Electronic Encyclopedia for all information relating to "espionage." You might be writing a paper for school, be conducting research for an article you are writing, or just be fascinated with spies. Whatever reason you have, Electronic Encyclopedia will provide you with the information you need.

Once you have determined the search word you want to use, you must enter the search word into the search window and press the ENTER key. Within three to five seconds the screen will change, listing all the references found during the search. Each listing will briefly describe the citation's content and length. Depending on the search word that you pick, you may have from one to over 35 different citations, each numbered for your referral.

Once this basic search for references is found, you can have each citation either displayed on your screen or printed out on paper. These features are discussed in the next tutorial segment. Right now, let's go through an actual example of how you can use Electronic Encyclopedia to search for citations for the search word "espionage."

**Hands-on Practice** If you do not already have the search window displayed on the video display terminal in front of you, load Electronic Encyclopedia and use the main menu to go to the search window. If you don't remember how, see page 38.

Now you are ready to conduct your first one-word search using Electronic Encyclopedia.

Step 1. Type the word ESPIONAGE in the search window and press the RETURN key. See sample screen below.

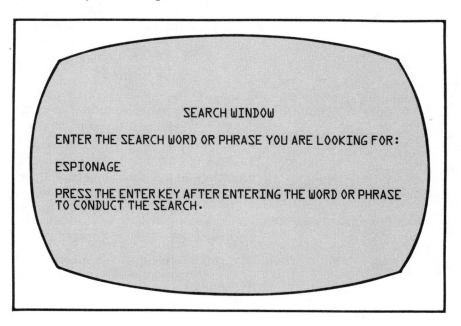

SEARCH WINDOW

ENTER THE SEARCH WORD OR PHRASE YOU ARE LOOKING FOR:

ESPIONAGE

PRESS THE ENTER KEY AFTER ENTERING THE WORD OR PHRASE TO CONDUCT THE SEARCH.

Step 2  After about three seconds, the search is complete and the screen changes, displaying all the citations Electronic Encyclopedia found for the search word "espionage." See the screen below.

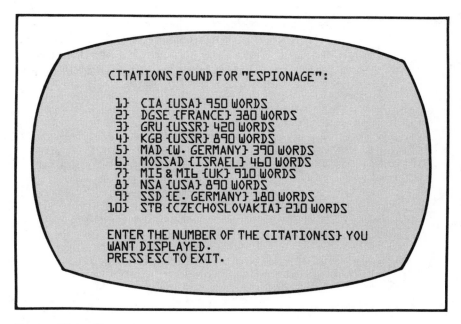

CITATIONS FOUND FOR "ESPIONAGE":

    1}   CIA {USA} 950 WORDS
    2}   DGSE {FRANCE} 380 WORDS
    3}   GRU {USSR} 420 WORDS
    4}   KGB {USSR} 890 WORDS
    5}   MAD {W. GERMANY} 390 WORDS
    6}   MOSSAD {ISRAEL} 460 WORDS
    7}   MI5 & MI6 {UK} 910 WORDS
    8}   NSA {USA} 890 WORDS
    9}   SSD {E. GERMANY} 180 WORDS
   10}   STB {CZECHOSLOVAKIA} 210 WORDS

ENTER THE NUMBER OF THE CITATION{S} YOU WANT DISPLAYED.
PRESS ESC TO EXIT.

Step 3   What you see on the screen are all the
          citations Electronic Encyclopedia has for
          the search word "espionage." Because we
          don't want to display any of the articles
          at this time (we'll save this for the next
          segment), press the ESC key to leave the
          current screen and return you to a blank
          search window.

Now that you have seen how to conduct a one-word search, try the following exercises for additonal practice. Once the citations are displayed, use the ESC key to start over again. Wait until the next tutorial segment to try displaying the articles. Besides trying the exercises listed, don't be afraid to try some of your own. Once you feel comfortable with entering search words and displaying the citations, you can move on to the next segment.

**Practical Exercises** Try entering the following search words. The correct results are displayed at the bottom of this box. [To save space, the answers are not displayed in this example.]
1)   Brazil
2)   Cat
3)   Computer
4)   Man
5)   Psychology

**Summary**
• One-word searches are the most common type of searches you will make.
• Enter your search word by typing in the word in the search window and pressing the ENTER key.
• Within several seconds after the search word is entered, all the citations, along with the number of words in each article, are displayed on the window. Use the ESC key to exit the citations and return to the search window.

**Lawford & Associates**

While working on the first draft of the tutorial section, Jill runs into a small problem concerning how the program prints reports. The preliminary version she has of the program does not have the printing feature fully implemented. She calls David to explain the problem. After getting David's answer, Jill fills him in about her progress on the preliminary draft.

"Once I get the tutorial complete, the rest of the manual will be easy. I think the most time-consuming part of writing the manual is thinking up realistic and practical examples."

"As simple as this program is, Jill, I don't think you will need too many examples. Besides, extra examples mean a longer and more expensive manual."

"Yes, but you have to remember that most of the users will be beginners and may need the extra practice to gain confidence in using the program. Besides the fully detailed examples, I'm including plenty of exercises. They take less space in the manual than examples, and since they're somewhat separated from the main body of the text, advanced users can skip them."

"I don't remember discussing adding exercises in the manual. I thought one or two examples for each operational feature of the program would be enough. This isn't a full-feature accounting program, you know."

"I know we didn't discuss exercises earlier, but as I was writing the manual outline, and now the tutorial itself, I thought it seemed wise to add them. They don't take up much space and I think they add a lot to the manual to make the program easier to use. How about including them in the preliminary version of the manual you're going to use in beta-testing, and see what kind of reaction we get. If the test results indicate that they're unnecessary, I can take them out for the final version."

"I'll go along with that. But you have to remember that my budget is tight and the cost of the manual has to be kept at a minimum."

"I'm aware of that. I have to get back to work. See you Monday."

# 8. How to Write Reference Sections

Typically when a student is assigned to write a term paper, the encyclopedia becomes his main source of information. Because it provides brief but adequate facts, quickly and accurately, it may be the only source of reference material most students need. Further research in books and magazines is time-consuming, and only the most devoted students take the time. Who would want to spend hours looking up obscure references in journals when all you have to do is spend ten minutes looking up the same subject in an encyclopedia?

Like an encyclopedia, the reference section of a software user manual contains a compendium of information about the use of the software. When a user needs to know something quickly about the program he is using, he doesn't want to wade through the tutorial, which is designed for intitial training. He wants to find complete information quickly and easily. This is the purpose of including a reference section in a user manual.

Unlike the tutorial, the reference section is not intended to be read from front to back, but rather to be referred to when the need arises. Users might want to read parts of it to familiarize themselves further with material they learned in the tutorial, or they may need to refer to it if they forget something at any time they are using the program. Some advanced users may skip the tutorial and read portions of the reference section to learn how to use the program. Although this is not the best way to learn a program, some users prefer to take their own approach to learning, and you as a manual writer must take this possibility into consideration.

## When to Use Reference Sections

In most user manuals a reference section is recommended for the convenience of the user. It is not absolutely mandatory, because the user can flip through the tutorial for information, but most users have come to expect reference sections in manuals. As a rule, you *should* include a reference section if your manual meets any of the following conditions.

• If the operation of the program is complex and it is unlikely that the user will be able to remember all of the commands and operations.

• If the program is used infrequently and the user is apt to forget how to operate any of its features.

- If the program has many advanced features that may need additional explanation not provided by the tutorial.
- If there are many people (with different skill levels) that use the program on a regular basis.

## Two Types of Reference Sections

Unlike the tutorial section, which follows the same structured format from manual to manual, the reference section can take two different forms. The format you choose depends on your audience and the software application. Use the following suggestions as a starting point for writing your own reference sections.

1. If the software:
   a. is heavily command-oriented, in other words, if the program requires many typed-in commands to make the program work, or
   b. is a programming language with many commands and statements, or
   c. is similar to a programming language (in that there are many commands or statements), such as many database programs,
   and if the users are either:
   a. intermediates, or
   b. experienced,
then consider a reference section that follows a dictionary-style approach. Arrange the section in alphabetical order by command, or statement, or function if appropriate. If the "definitions" of the "listings" are long, then keep one listing per page; otherwise you can include more than one listing on a page, much as in a real dictionary. Include with the definition and explanation of the listing any special rules that apply to it, and consider including an example of how the listing is used in the program.

In most cases, this style of reference section is best suited for software that is complex and requires the user regularly to look up listings for detailed information. (See Figure 8-1.)

## Figure 8-1
## Dictionary Style

*The dictionary-style format in a reference section is especially useful when a program has many commands, such as the description of the LIST command below from the BASIC programming language.*

### LIST Command
**Purpose:**
Used to display all or part of a program on the video display screen.

**Format:**
LIST, LIST[n], LIST[-n], LIST[n-], LIST[n-n]

**Comments:**
You have five options with the LIST Command:

LIST displays all the program lines currently residing in memory. When used, it quickly scrolls the program on the video display screen. The scrolling can be interrupted temporarily by pressing CTRL-NUMLOCK and resumed by pressing any key. The scrolling can be permanently stopped by pressing CTRL-BREAK. For example:

    LIST

displays every line of your entire program on the video display screen.

LIST[n] displays only one line from your program. For example:

    LIST100

displays the program line 100 on the video display screen.

LIST[-n] displays all the program lines in your program up to the line number you have specified. For example:

    LINE-100

displays every line in your program up to line number 100 on your video display screen.

LIST[n-] displays all the program lines in your program from the line number you have specified to the end of the program. For example:

    List250-

displays all the program lines in your program from line number 250 on.

LIST[n-n] displays all the program lines in your program between the line numbers you have specified. For example:

    LIST250-1000

displays all the program lines in your program between line numbers 250 and 1000.

Writing Software User Manuals

2. If the software:
   a. is menu-driven, or
   b. has few typed-in commands, or
   c. features operations that are easily grouped into distinct func-
      tions, such as data entry, report printing, and so on,
and if the users are:
   a. beginners, or
   b. intermediates, or
   c. experienced

then consider following an encyclopedia-style approach to writing your reference section. Rather than adhering to a strictly "look up the information approach" used with the dictionary-style format, the encyclopedia approach is more comprehensive in content and lends itself more to reading and studying in depth. In most cases, the content of the reference section is arranged alphabetically by subject. What you essentially do is recast the information you wrote about in the manual's tutorial, but instead of taking a teaching approach with everything spelled out step by step, you take a more direct approach and summarize the information clearly and concisely.

For example, if the user wanted to know how to print a report, he would look up the section on "Printing" and find a brief but complete description of how to print reports with the program.

Begin writing each segment of the reference section with a statement of purpose. This one- or two-sentence statement briefly summarizes what the rest of the segment is about and quickly tells the reader if he is reading the right portion. Often when a user is looking up a particular operation, he is not exactly sure what he needs to do. His search is even more complicated if the program offers similar options that might be confused with each other. The summary helps the user find the information he needs quickly and efficiently.

The encyclopedia-style approach to reference section writing is the one most commonly found in user manuals because it is flexible and fits most audience needs and most software applications. (See Figure 8-2.)

A variation of this approach is not only to include the information in your tutorial in the reference section, but also to include the information from all the other sections of your manual, such as the Introduction and Getting Started. You still follow the same encyclopedia-style and all the information is grouped together in a similar format. This style can be used if you think a good many of the users are experienced and will not want to waste time going over the other sections of the manual that were written for beginners. While this is redundant for you as the writer, and more costly to produce, it makes a manual that is very flexible for a wide variety of potential users.

**Figure 8-2**
**Encyclopedia Style**
*The encyclopedia-style reference section usually is divided into functional areas (such as printing above), and reiterates tutorial information, but more briefly, and not in a step-by-step format.*

## Printing the Search Report
**Purpose:**
How to print the results of a search you made with Electronic Encyclopedia.

Once you have completed a search and gathered a number of articles on your subject of interest, you can print the articles, or portions of articles, for later use.

When you first designated what articles, or portions of articles, interested you, this information was stored in the computer's memory. Now that you want to print the results of your search, all you have to do is tell Electronic Encyclopedia that you want the search report printed.

### How to Print the Search Report
To print the search report, choose the "Print Search Report" option from the Main Menu. The screen will change and ask you what type of format you want the search report printed in. (See screen below.)

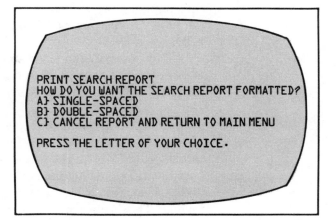

```
PRINT SEARCH REPORT
HOW DO YOU WANT THE SEARCH REPORT FORMATTED?
A} SINGLE-SPACED
B} DOUBLE-SPACED
C} CANCEL REPORT AND RETURN TO MAIN MENU

PRESS THE LETTER OF YOUR CHOICE.
```

If you press either *A* or *B*, the search report will automatically be printed. Pressing choice *C* cancels the report option and returns you back to the main menu.

## Guidelines for Writing Reference Sections

Whichever of the above reference section formats you choose, the following guidelines should be applied, as needed, to meet the needs of the users:

• Slant the material to meet the needs of your audience and the software application. Beginning users need more explanation and examples of a program's use whereas advanced users often need more technical information to get the most out of the program.

• Divide the material, as you did with the tutorial, into one idea, point, concept, or technique at a time. Whatever approach you take in the reference section, don't confuse the user by trying to present too much information at one time.

• Especially for novices, but also for experienced users, consider using examples and illustrations to help get the information across as clearly and interestingly as possible.

• Be as complete as possible when explaining the material. Don't force the user to look up several separate subjects to find related information.

• Pick and follow a consistent format for the reference section. This reassures the user that he will always be able to find the information he needs quickly and easily.

• As with the tutorial, test the reference section after it is written to ensure that all material, examples, and illustrations are 100 percent accurate.

## Steps to Writing Reference Sections

Like writing any part of the user manual, writing the reference section takes several distinct steps. No matter which format you choose, you will want to follow these steps.

1. Plan the reference section along with the rest of the manual, keeping in mind that you want to fashion it to the user.

2. Once you have decided on the format to follow, outline the reference section with the rest of the manual, including all the relevant material. You might have to rewrite the outline several times to ensure that everything is covered.

3. Writing the first draft is your next step. Waiting to write the reference section last is a good idea. It gives you a chance to see exactly what information will be included in the rest of the manual. In many cases when writing the reference section, you will only have to summarize what you have already written in the rest of the manual.

4. The rest of the steps for writing the reference section follow along with writing the rest of the manual. See Chapter 9 for more information.

## Lawford & Associates

Jill has finished the preliminary draft of the Home Mortgage Calculator user manual. At their weekly meeting, David looks the manual over, asks Jill various questions, and makes suggestions for changes.

"My biggest problem with this manual is the reference section," says David after reading the manual. "I don't think it's necessary. I know we decided to include it in our earlier discussions, but now that I see it, I think it's a waste of time. The tutorial covers the same information, making the reference section redundant."

"But aren't all the reference sections more or less redundant? They're supposed to be a repeat the manual's contents, but in an abbreviated form, designed for easy retrieval of information."

"I know, but this manual is so small in the first place. Don't you think that users can use the index to locate any information in the tutorial just as easily as looking it up in a reference section?"

"In most cases you're probably right, but there are two benefits you're forgetting. First, experienced users don't usually like to wade through tutorials designed for beginners. It's a waste of time for them and they prefer to read quickly through a reference section to grasp the important information. Second, novice users who use the program occasionally often forget how to use some features of the program and reading an abbreviated reference section is faster and more convenient than rereading a tutorial."

"But don't you think that your two examples consist of a relatively small percentage of the audience for this program?"

"Perhaps. You're the expert on the program's audience. But it's my feeling that the extra expense of including a reference section will be more than made up by having a well-rounded manual, complete in all aspects. You're right that the reference section may not always be used, but I think including one may make the difference for some prospective customers when they examine the manual. If they see that it looks complete, it might swing a sale that might not be made if the manual were incomplete."

"That reminds me of another point, Jill. Software reviewers often look for manual completeness, and including a reference section may help us get better reviews. Okay, you've made your point. Let's go with the reference section. Overall the manual looks good and I'm ready to use it for the upcoming beta-testing of Home Mortgage Calculator."

# 9. Writing Your Manual from First Draft to Final Copy

It's a scene you hear about time and time again. The writer sits at his desk staring at a blank piece of paper (or a green phosphorescent video display screen), unable to write anything because of the dreaded malady, writer's block. Few writers can escape its grip. It affects novelists and short story writers, newspaper and magazine writers, even manual writers.

Regrettably, the actual writing of a manual is the most feared part of manual writing. This fear is a result of misconceptions held by many beginning writers. They think that after some preliminary, brief outlining they can just sit down and start writing a manual.

By now you should have learned that manual writing is not one step, but many small, comprehensible, and easy-to-complete steps that build upon each other. Does this sound familiar? It should. Just as we want to break down the instructional material into easily digestible chunks for the reader, we must do the same for ourselves when writing the manual.

Although the actual writing of the manual is the largest part of manual writing, it represents an average of less than 25 percent of the total time. The rest of the time is spent planning, outlining, rewriting, testing, and proofreading the manual. The better you prepare for writing the first draft of the manual, the easier you will find it to write. If you have ever programmed before, you will realize that manual writing is similar to following structured programming techniques, with more time spent planning the program than actually writing it.

This chapter outlines the process of writing the manual, from getting ready, to writing the first draft, to rewriting the draft into a preliminary version, to testing the manual for user clarity and ease of use, to polishing the final draft, to proofreading the final version. At the end of the chapter is the finished manual of Lawford & Associates.

**Getting Ready**

Before you begin writing the first draft of your manual, you must have the necessary tools and information at hand. The requirements vary from writer to writer and from manual to manual, but the following list should be a good start.

• **The Outline.** If you have not yet prepared a detailed outline of the manual, stop and prepare it now. First drafts are written on the basis of the outline. As was discussed in Chapter 5, the outline ensures proper organization, which in turn helps to make your manual understandable to the reader. If there is no outline, writer's block or an incomprehensible manual will result.

• **Microcomputer and Software.** You must have the software you are writing the manual for and the appropriate microcomputer(s). If the package operates on more than one microcomputer and if the operations on each are slightly different but only one manual is being written, you must have access to all models. Even though you have your notes on the operation of the software, you will want to verify previous findings and work out examples and exercises on each machine to ensure absolute compatability of your written instructions.

• **Word Processing Software.** While it is not mandatory to do so, writing your first draft using word processing software saves substantial time and effort. Not only does it increase writing speed, it saves considerable time later when rewriting is done. Also helpful, but not required, is spelling checker and writing style analysis software. While they don't catch all errors, they can help you save much proofreading time.

• **Illustration Supplies.** At this stage you will want to do rough sketches of diagrams or illustrations. At minimum you need pencil, paper, eraser, and a straight edge. If you have experience, you might want to use drawing or drafting tools to assist your work.

**The First Draft**

A first draft is just that—a draft. Its purpose is not to be the final, polished version, but rather a working form of the manual. Writing the first draft brings to your attention many details that you may have not considered before, often causing you to rethink what you want to say. Trying to write with perfect style at the same time is nearly impossible, so concentrate on the content and organization of the material and worry about style later.

Below is a suggested procedure for writing your first draft. Use it only as a guideline. After you gain some experience, you will probably develop your own approach. No two writers write a first draft the same way.

1. Write the first draft in the standard manuscript format. That is, allow generous outside margins, and double-space on one side of a sheet of 8½x11-inch paper. Left-justify headings and leave two or more spaces between the heading and the text. This format makes it easy for you to revise the draft in the later writing stages. Also, if your manual is to be typeset, this is the format the typesetter expects the manuscript to be in. Also, if you decide to format and print the manual with word processing software, do so only after the manuscript is completely done. Otherwise, you will only waste time reformatting the text as your revise it.

2. If you are using a word processor, have each section of the manual

in a separate text file. This system keeps any one file from being too long and awkward to handle. You may also want to keep one file per diskette, especially if the files are large or the storage capacity of your disk drives is small.

3. Write the draft in any order you feel most comfortable with. The outline you prepared may direct you to a particular starting point, such as the Getting Started or Introduction section. Where you begin depends on you and the type of manual you are writing. Some writers find it easier to start with the hardest sections first and save the easiest one until later rather than writing the manual in its finished order.

4. Carefully follow your outline, using it as your guideline to writing. As you get to examples, exercises, and illustrations, rough them out and be sure they work; you don't necessarily have to put them in final form. Don't let anything hang you up as you write the first draft. If you get stuck on something, skip it for now and continue with something else. You can come back later to figure it out, and perhaps you will see the problem in a new light.

5. Write the manual "quick and dirty," not worrying about spelling, grammar, or style if you don't want to. Concentrate on getting *something* down; perfection can come later.

6. After you have finished each section, if you have the software, run it through spelling checker and writing style analysis programs to catch obvious errors. Doing this will make later revision a little easier.

**Lawford & Associates First Draft**

Below is the first draft of the "How to Use This Manual" segment of the Introduction of the Home Mortgage Calculator Manual. It was written with a word processor in the standard manuscript format and has not been proofread or formatted in any special way. Compare this first draft to the final version of this segment found in the finished manual at the end of this chapter.

### How to Use This Manual
To get the most good out of Home Mortgage Caluclator, you should read this manual carefully. It will answer any questions you might have about Home Mortgage Calculator's operation.

It is assumed that you are familiar with the operation of your computer and have read your computer manuals. If not, do so now before you begin using Home Mortgage Calculator.

### Getting Started
After you read this introduction, your next step is to prepare Home Mortgage Calculator. You will learn how to do this in the section titled "Getting Started".

### Tutorial
Once the program has been prepared, you can begin the tutorial. It

leads you step by step through the use of the program. Not only does the tutorial show you how to use the program but it gives you practical examples with the results so you can see how you are doing. The tutorial should not take longer than 1 hour to finish.

### Reference Section

Once you have finished the tutorial, you are ready to use Home Mortgage Manager. But for additional help, should you need it, the reference section contains information about the program arranged in a good format. Use the reference section, instead of the tutorial, to look up operation questions you have about using the program.

### Appendix

In the appendix you will find detailed information on error messages, how home mortgage calculator makes its calculations, and a technical discussion about the program.

### Glossary and Index

The glossary is designed to help you understand the computer words in the manual. Use it if you don't understand any term. The index provides easy access to information located throughout the manual.

### Quick Reference Card

Included with the manual is a quick reference card that summarizes the operation of Home Mortgage Calculator. You may find it easier to use than the manual when you have a simple question about the program's operation.

## Rewriting the First Draft

The worst is over. After the first draft is written, everything else is downhill. The first draft helped you to think about the manual's content and organization, bringing up points you probably did not consider when you outlined the manual. As you added new information in the draft, it was inevitable that the manual's organization and clarity suffered. Perhaps a new point added in one section affects another, which therefore needs to be updated. This is the essence of rewriting.

Rewriting, either minor or major in scope, is always necessary after the first draft. It gives you the chance to make any corrections you need to refine the organization of the manual. You may have to do more than one rewrite on particular sections or parts of sections. This depends on you and the difficulty of the corrections. Here are some suggestions for rewriting the first draft.

**1.** Print out the entire first draft on paper (if you are using a typewriter, you already have a printout), using the standard manuscript format. Review your writing and make comments on the copy as you proceed. Write directly on the paper, so you can refer to it as you make the corrections for the next version. This is where a word processor comes in handy; it eliminates retyping of text that does not need revision.

**2.** Start the editing and rewriting from the beginning of the manual, and proceed sequentially until it is complete. This method helps to ensure consistency among the various sections and gives you a good perspective on the entire manual.

**3.** Concentrate your revision on content and organization, with some consideration to style. Leave the style to a later stage, as it is easier to do one thing at a time.

**4.** Once you have a revised version of the manual stored on diskette, again use the spelling checker and writing style software to locate problems and correct them. Your rewriting is bound to introduce some new problems. If you have been using a typewriter instead of a word processor, you may want to retype a completely new set of pages to start out fresh.

**Testing the Manual**

By this stage, the manual should be almost in its final form. Before the polishing touches are made, however, you must take the time to test the manual for clarity, usefulness, accuracy, and completeness. Ideally, this should be done through beta-testing of the software conducted by the programmer or software publisher. This is a formal method of testing the software and manual under realistic conditions and usually does not involve the manual writer. Beta-testing of software is beyond the scope of this manual, but if you are faced with the situation of testing the manual by yourself, you might consider following the suggestions listed below. They are not formal and could not be called scientific, but they should help you catch most of the potential problems users might have.

**1.** Photocopy at least six copies of the manual in manuscript form. They are to be used by people you choose to evaluate the manual. Also write an evaluation instruction sheet stating exactly what about the manual you want evaluated, and how. Because you are testing the manual for clarity, ease of use, and accuracy, tailor your questions to elicit such information. For example, you might ask the user to mark words or passages in the manual that are not clear, or to mark illustrations or other information that does not correspond exactly to the program, or to make suggestions for improvement. You will have to tailor the questions to the unique aspects of the program and manual.

**2.** Next, choose at least three members from the target audience of the manual and software, the programmer of the software, an expert in microcomputers who is unfamiliar with the software and manual, and at least one professional writer (or student writer).

**3.** If possible, try to set up a situation where the three audience members can get together all at once and actually use the manual along with the software. Have each one work individually. While they read the manual and go through the tutorial to learn the software, observe them and take notes on how they proceed. Try to see where they have problems, and if they ask you questions because they do not understand something in the manual, make a note of them. You might have to schedule several sessions for them to complete the instruction period. Have them mark the manual as they go along, using the evaluation instructions you developed for them. After they are done, orally interview them as a group; have them evaluate the manual, telling you where they had problems and would suggest changes. You will thus have both their oral and written comments. Compare these comments with your observations to see if they coincide. If they do not, try to find out why. The users may not always mention where they had problems, either because they forgot or they are embarrassed.

**4.** Give each of the other three copies of the manual to the programmer, the microcomputer expert, and the writer. Have them make comments on it as they read it. If possible, have them also (even the programmer) use the manual and software together. Each of these three people will bring a different perspective to the manual, contributing invaluable suggestions.

**5.** Collect all the information you gathered from the testing and organize it into one comprehensive form for use in the next step.

**6.** If you have a Quick Reference Card, don't forget to test it, too.

## Polishing the Manuscript

You are almost done. The testing you just did will suggest some changes to your manual. If you did a good job of writing before the testing, the changes you make should be few and easy to make. If your planning was inadequate, or the testing revealed major problems, you might have to skip back a step and do a complete rewrite. If so, you should test the manual again. From here on, it is assumed that the changes are minimal.

Unlike the rewriting stage, the polishing stage deals with words, sentences, and paragraphs. Now you will work to improve style where needed. Following the advice in Chapter 6 will further make your manual clearer and more interesting to read. You may want to follow the steps given below to polish your manuscript.

**1.** As you did earlier, print out the manual on paper to make editing and revision easier. Make all your corrections directly on the paper so you can later go back and correct the file with your word processor.

**2.** Concentrate on individual words, sentences, and paragraphs and the way they fit together. Have a dictionary, thesaurus, and style manual handy to refer to. Change words for more exact meaning, or rewrite sentences as necessary to conform to the suggestions in Chapter 6. Reading the text out loud to yourself or others often makes it easier to concentrate on individual words.

**3.** After you have corrected the word processing file, run the text again through a spelling checker and writing style program one more time to catch any unseen problems.

## Proofreading the Manual

You've almost made it. After polishing the manuscript, you still must check one more time, watching for the following:

- Spelling or typographical errors
- Improper grammar
- Inconsistency in spelling, word usage, abbreviations, and so on
- Errors in the rough drafts of illustrations and in their placement in the text
- Whether examples and exercises work as expected

If possible, get someone else to do the proofreading. Have him follow your style sheet (if you have one) and carefully check out the manual. This should not be done quickly, but methodically. Small errors may frustrate the reader, ruining any attempt you have made to organize the manual in a clear manner. Once all errors are corrected, the manuscript is ready to be sent to the typesetters, typeset yourself, or formatted and printed using your own word processor and printer.

## Lawford & Associates

At this point Jill has written the first draft of the Home Mortgage Calculator manual and listened to the comments of David about it. Now before the manual is ready to be included with the beta-test version of the program, Jill must rewrite the manual, incorporating David's suggestions and further refining the manual's content and organization. Her next week is spent rewriting and preparing the manual for beta-testing, which is to start the following Monday.

On Monday she delivers the manual, and David and Jill have their weekly meeting in the morning instead of the afternoon. Jill learns that the beta-testing is being conducted by a college professor consulting for Lawford & Associates and she does not have to participate. A summary of the test results will be given to her after the testing is complete so that she can incorporate the new information into the manual.

Since the beta-testing will take a week, Jill spends her time talking to printers around town about their services and prices.

The week over, she meets with David on Monday and gets the results of the testing. Jill spends the next week rewriting the manual, employing the comments made by the college professor and polishing the manual into its final draft.

On the following Monday she gives the final copy to David and to a friend to proofread. David is happy with the manual and gives Jill the go-ahead to contact printers and have them bid to design and print the manual. Once it's proofread, Jill makes the final changes to the manual and the written part is complete.

## For More Information on Word Processing

If you want to learn more about word processing, consider reading one of these books: *Writing in the Computer Age* by Andrew Fluegelman and Jeremy Joan Hewes (Doubleday & Co., 1983), or *Writing with a Word Processor* by William Zinsser (Harper & Row, 1983).

If you are looking for word processing software, I would recommend a "high-power" word processor such as WORDSTAR by Micropro or MICROSOFT WORD by Microsoft. Both of these programs include many powerful editing and text-formatting capabilities that make writing easy.

# Home Mortgage Calculator User Manual

**Lawford & Associates**

# Customer Service

If you ever have any problems using this program, feel free to call our toll-free customer service phone number.

Customer Service Phone Number:
(800)555-1234
Weekdays, 9:00 a.m. - 5:00 p.m. CST

First Edition, April 1984

Lawford & Associates
P.O. Box 4585
Springfield, MO 65808

Program written by David Lawford
Manual written by Jill Bates

Trademark Acknowledgements:
Columbia is a trademark of Columbia Data Products, Inc.
COMPAQ is a trademark of COMPAQ Computer Corporation.
Hyperion is a trademark of Bytech Hyperion.
IBM is a trademark of International Business Machines Corporation.

# Table of Contents

## 1. INTRODUCTION
How to Use This Manual
Following Examples
Terminology
Overview of Program
Program Control
How to Cope with Error Messages
Summary

## 2. GETTING STARTED
What You Need to Get Started
Preparing the Working Copy
Printer Setup

## 3. TUTORIAL
Introduction
Loading Home Mortgage Calculator
Using the Calculator Screen
Displaying and Printing Comparison Tables
Exiting Home Mortgage Calculator

## 4. REFERENCE
Introduction
How to Use the Reference Section
Loading Home Mortgage Calculator
Using the Calculator Screen
Displaying and Printing Comparison Tables
Exiting Home Mortgage Calculator

**Appendix A:** Error Messages *(Abbreviated list—Ed.)*
**Appendix B:** How Home Mortgage Calculator Makes Its Calculations *(Not included—Ed.)*
**Appendix C:** Technical Notes *(Not included—Ed.)*

**Glossary**

**Index**

# Preface

Welcome to Home Mortgage Calculator.

Home Mortgage Calculator is a computer program designed to help you make informed decisions about home mortgage financing.

With Home Mortgage Calculator you can:

• Calculate any of the following amounts: house purchase price, percentage down payment, loan term, annual interest rate, or monthly mortgage payment.
• See what your monthly mortgage payments would be at various interest rates and purchase prices.
• See what your monthly mortgage payments would be at various interest rates and loan terms.

Home Mortgage Calculator's benefits include:

• It provides the information you need to make informed decisions about home mortgage financing. You no longer have to depend on real estate agents or lending institutions to calculate monthly home mortgage payments for you.
• You can experiment with various combinations of purchase price, down payment, loan term, interest rate, and monthly payment that meet your needs, not the needs of a lending institution.
• Home Mortgage Calculator is easy to use and learn. In less than one hour of practice Home Mortgage Calculator will be working for you.

To use Home Mortgage Calculator you will need the following computer equipment:

• An IBM, IBM XT or IBM-compatible personal computer.
• A minimum of 64K of random access memory (RAM).
• At least one 160K floppy disk drive.
• A monochrome or color video display terminal.
• The disk operating system (DOS 1.1 or 2.0) used by your computer.
• A printer is optional.
• Home Mortgage Calculator is not copy protected and works with any hard disk drive.

The manual is divided into these sections:
• Table of Contents
• Introduction
• Getting Started
• Tutorial
• Reference Section
• Appendix
• Glossary
• Index
• Quick Reference Card (separate from manual).

# Introduction to Home Mortgage Calculator

This section presents an overview of Home Mortgage Calculator. It provides an overview of how Home Mortgage Calculator works along with suggestions on how to get the most out of this manual.

Covered in this section:

• How to Use This Manual
• Following Examples
• Terminology
• Overview of Program
• Program Control
• How to Cope with Error Messages
• Summary

## How to Use This Manual

To get the most out of Home Mortgage Calculator, you must read this manual carefully. It will answer any questions you might have about Home Mortgage Calculator's operation.

It is assumed that you are familiar with the operation of your computer and have read your operations and DOS manuals. If you have not read these manuals, take the time now to do so before you begin using Home Mortgage Calculator.

## Getting Started

After you read this introduction, your next step is to prepare Home Mortgage Calculator for use. You will learn how to do this in the section titled "Getting Started."

## Tutorial

Once the program has been prepared, you can begin the tutorial. This section leads you step by step through the use of Home Mortgage Calculator. Not only does the tutorial show you how to use this program, it also gives you practical examples of every operation with the correct results, so you can see how you are doing. The tutorial should not take longer than one-half hour to complete.

## Reference Section

After you have completed the tutorial, you are ready to use Home Mortgage Calculator. However, for additional assistance, should you need it, the reference section contains information about the program arranged in an easy-to-find format. Use the reference section instead of the tutorial to look up operation questions you have about using Home Mortgage Calculator once you have become familiar with it.

## Appendix

In the appendix you will find detailed information on error messages, how Home Mortgage Calculator actually makes its calculations, and a technical discussion about the program. This is optional reading. *(Most of the appendix is not included.— Ed.)*

## Glossary & Index

The glossary lists many computer-related terms. Use it if you don't understand a term found in this manual. The index provides easy access to information located throughout the manual.

## Quick Reference Card

Accompanying the manual is a quick reference card that summarizes the operation of Home Mortgage Calculator. You may find it easier to use than the manual when you have a simple question about the program's operation.

## Following Examples

Throughout this manual many step-by-step procedures and examples are given. Each of these requires that you type certain commands, eliciting various responses from your computer. To make it easy for you to follow these steps, this manual adheres to the following conventions about keyboard entry and computer responses.

## Entering Commands

Whenever an example is given in this manual, the commands you are to enter via the keyboard will be in all capital letters and indented. Below is an example.

To start Home Mortgage Calculator, type in the command: HMC after the system prompt and press the: ENTER key to start the program.

While the commands are always in capital letters, this does not mean you have to enter the commands using capital letters. Home Mortgage Calculator accepts commands either in lowercase or uppercase letters.

Also note above that there are two different types of commands. The first, "HMC," above, is a command that is typed letter by letter into the keyboard. But

"ENTER" is a key to be pressed. One-key commands such as this are enclosed by a picture of a key. All examples tell you whether to type in the command or press a key. After some practice, you will instinctively know what to do.

## Recognizing Computer Responses

There are two different ways that computer responses are shown in this manual. The most common is to have the response indented on the page like this using regular uppercase and lowercase letters. While these responses do not fill an entire screen, they are surrounded by a smaller version of a screen so that you always know that what is printed on the page should also be displayed on the screen.

You have accidentally entered a letter(s) for one of the financial terms. Numbers only are accepted. Please find your error and correct it. Continue using the program as before.

The second way the manual shows computer responses is by showing a full-size picture of the screen as it is displayed on the video display terminal. See Figure 1.

## Terminology

The terminology used by Home Mortgage Calculator and this manual is designed to be familiar and easy to understand. Because some people may not be familiar with all the terms unique to Home Mortgage Calculator, however, the following list of definitions is provided.

At the back of this manual is a glossary with additional defined words. It includes words that are not unique to the program but are found in most computer manuals; these are provided should you not be familiar with computer terminology.

**Annual Interest Rate.** The amount of the annual interest rate (or annual percentage rate) charged by a lending institution for a home mortgage loan.

**Box.** Refers to a rectangular box of light on the screen. All information entered into Home Mortgage Calculator is entered in these boxes.

**Calculator Screen.** This is the heart of Home Mortgage Calculator and is the "control panel" of the program. It is divided into two windows. The top window is where financing terms are entered, calculations occur, and results are displayed. The bottom window is used to display comparison tables.

**Comparison Table.** A table of possible monthly mortgage payments based on various combinations of financing terms.

**Financing Terms.** These are the numeric values that represent the purchase price, percentage down payment, loan term, annual interest rate, and monthly payment. For example: 55,000, 87,000, and 125,000 represent possible purchase prices; 10, 20, and 25 percent represent possible percentage down payments; 10, 20, and 30

years represent possible loan terms; 10, 12, and 18 percent represent possible annual interest rates; and 350, 480, and 880 represent possible monthly payments.

**Loan Term.** The total number of years the mortgage will be financed by the lending institution. For example: 20 years, 30 years.

**Monthly Payment.** The monthly payment that is made to the lending institution for the term of the mortgage loan. This one figure includes both the interest and principal amounts.

**Percentage Down Payment.** The percentage of the purchase price that is to be the down payment for the mortgage loan. For example: 10 percent, 15 percent.

**Program Diskette.** This is the original floppy diskette you get when you purchase Home Mortgage Calculator. It contains the various programs that make up Home Mortgage Calculator. The program diskette should not be employed in everyday use but, once copied, should be stored in a safe location.

**Purchase Price.** The negotiated price of the house that is being considered for purchase; the price you will be paying the seller for the house.

**Screen.** The information displayed on your video display screen at any one point in time.

# Overview of Program

**Working Copy.** This is the copy of the original program diskette of Home Mortgage Calculator you make to employ in everyday use.

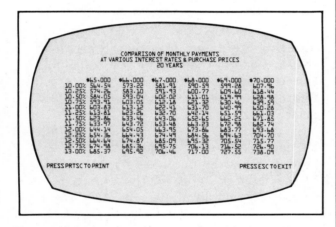

**Figure 1.** *Sample Screen Response*

Why Use Home Mortgage Calculator?

Home Mortgage Calculator is a personal productivity program designed to help you make informed decisions about home mortgage financing.

As a home buyer, you are usually at the mercy of real estate agents or bankers when it comes to calculating monthly mortgage payments. You may know what monthly mortgage amount you are comfortable paying, but you don't know what combination of purchase price, down payment, loan term, and interest rate make up that amount.

Different combinations of these financing terms add up to what you can afford to pay. Home Mortgage Calculator is designed to make it easy for you to examine and experiment with many different combinations of financing terms so that you can decide for yourself what combination meets your needs.

With a real estate agent or banker, you are usually limited to the information they want to provide, and this may not be to your advantage.

Home Mortgage Calculator allows you to take all the time you want to make the best financial decision by presenting all the information you need to make that decision.

**The Calculator Screen**
After Home Mortgage Calculator is loaded and running, you are presented with what is called the calculator screen. It is divided into two windows. The top window, or calculator window, is where financing terms are entered, calculations take place, and

results are displayed. The bottom window, or comparison window, is used to create comparison tables.

**The Calculator Window**
Displayed in the calculator window are these financing terms:

• Purchase Price
• Percentage Down Payment
• Loan Term
• Annual Interest Rate
• Monthly Payment

After each of the financing terms is a box where you enter the numeric value for that financing term.

All you have to do is enter the proper amount for four of the five financing options and the financing term left blank will instantly be calculated after you press the F10 key (CALCULATE key)

**Experimenting with Financing Terms**
You can experiment with a variety of financing options. For example, if you want to calculate the monthly mortgage payment, fill in the other four financing terms and press the F10 key; the monthly payment is instantly displayed.

Or say you know that you can afford a monthly payment of $650.00 and you want to find out the maximum purchase price you can afford for a house, when you know the percent down payment, loan term, and interest rate you can afford. Fill in the appropriate amounts, press F10, and the maximum amount you can afford, given the

financing terms you gave, will be displayed on the screen.

You can experiment as much as you wish, using trial and error to determine the best combination of financing options to meet your needs. If you have a printer you can print the calculator screen on a sheet of paper.

**The Comparison Window**
The bottom window on the calculator screen, the comparison window, lets you display two different types of comparison tables. These two tables make it easier for you to see and compare various mortgage financing options.

You decide which comparison table you want to see, and Home Mortgage Calculator takes the financing terms you entered in the calculator window and uses these figures to create the table. If you want to see another variation of the table, change the financing terms and a new table, using the new terms, is created and displayed.

The first comparison screen, titled "Comparison of Monthly Payments at Various Interest Rates & Purchase Prices," allows you to examine what monthly mortgage payment you would have to make assuming various combinations of interest rates and purchase prices.

The second comparison screen, titled "Comparison of Monthly Payments at Various Interest Rates & Loan Terms" allows you to examine what monthly mortgage payment you would have to make assuming various combinations of interest rates and loan terms.

## Program Control

When you are using the program, there are various commands that you can give by pressing keys. They are:

F1             **Jump Key.** Used to jump the cursor from one window on the calculator screen to the other.

F10            **Calculate key.** Used to calculate the unknown financing term.

ESC           **Escape key (Exit key).** Used to return to the calculator screen from the comparison table. Also, if you press ESC while at the calculator screen, you will exit the program and return to the operating system of your computer.

PRTSC      **Print Screen key.** Used to print either the calculator screen or the comparison tables.

ENTER      **Enter key.** Used to cause the computer to act on your previously entered command.

4←— 
—4›           **Tab key.** Used to move from one financing term to another. Each time you press it, the cursor will jump to the next one. Pressing the shift key and the tab key at the same time moves the cursor

to the previous financing term.

4←—          **Backspace key.** Used to correct errors. It moves the cursor one space back and erases any character in that space.

4 
4←— 
6 
—4›           **Cursor Control keys.** Used to correct keyboard entries. Moves the cursor left and right one character at a time without erasing any characters.

## How to Cope with Error Messages

There are two possible sources of errors when you are using Home Mortgage Calculator. Although everything has been done to prevent errors, you may still experience them from time to time. Here's how to cope with them.

**Program Errors**
Program errors are those that relate to how to you use the program. For example, instead of entering a numeric value for a financing term, you might accidentally enter a letter along with the other numbers making up your entry. If you were to press the F10 key to make a calculation, the program would give you an error message.

Program error messages have three parts:

•   An audible and visual cue
•   A description of the error
•   A solution to the error

If you made the above error, you would first hear a short beep from the computer and see the following error message appear at the bottom of the calculator screen:

You have accidentally entered a letter(s) in one of the financing terms. Only numbers are acceptable. Please find your error and correct it.

Continue using the program as before.

If you should get any error messages like this when using the program, just follow the instructions given. The error message disappears the next time you press the F10 key.

## Computer Errors

Computer error messages are given by the computer to you and don't follow the format illustrated above. They may result from problems from either your computer hardware or the floppy diskette you are using for the working copy of the program. Home Mortgage Calculator has no control over these error messages and you should refer to the appendix section of this manual for their solution should you encounter any. You can always tell the difference between the two types of errors because computer error messages don't display a solution to the error on your video display screen.

## Summary

•   Read the manual before using Home Mortgage Calculator.

•   Use the glossary if you don't understand all the terminology found in the manual.

•   The calculator screen is divided into two windows. The calculator window is used to enter financing term, make calculations, and display results. The comparison window is used to display comparison tables.

•   Program Control

F1 . . . . . . . Window JUMP key
F10 . . . . . . CALCULATE key
ESC . . . . . . EXIT key
ENTER . . . ENTER key
←—
—› . . . . . . . . TAB key
←— . . . . . . . BACKSPACE key
←—
4 . . . . . . . . . Moves cursor left
—›
6 . . . . . . . . . Moves cursor right

•   Two types of error messages: Program: Caused by user; error message with solution is displayed on screen.
Computer: Caused by computer; see appendix for solution.

# Getting Started

## What You Need to Get Started

• Any IBM-compatible computer. Specific computers known to work with Home Mortgage Calculator include:
  • IBM or IBM XT Personal Computer
  • Columbia Personal Computer
  • COMPAQ Portable Computer
  • Hyperion Portable Computer

• Computer must have a minimum of 64K of random access memory (RAM). Additional RAM is of no advantage with this program.
• At least one 160K floppy disk drive. 320K floppy disk drives or hard disk drives will also work. *(To save space, any further references to hard disks are eliminated from this manual.—Ed.)*
• Any monochrome or color video display terminal. Television sets are not recommended because of their poor resolution.
• The Disk Operating Systems (DOS 1.1 or DOS 2.0.) for your computer.

You will also need:

• One blank, formatted, 5¼-inch, single- or double-sided, double-density floppy diskette. Refer to your DOS manual if you have any questions on how to format a diskette. This will be used to make a working copy of Home Mortgage Calculator.
• The Home Mortgage Calculator program diskette.

Optional Equipment:

• Any parallel or serial printer that works with your computer. See instructions below for how to tell Home Mortgage Calculator which printer you have.

## Preparing the Working Copy

Before you can use Home Mortgage Calculator, you must first complete some preparatory steps. Once they are complete, you may begin the tutorial section of this manual.

Your first step is to make a working copy of the original Home Mortgage Calculator program diskette that came with this manual. This is done for two reasons:

1. Because floppy diskettes are susceptible to damage, it is unwise to use the original program diskette for regular use. If it is ever lost or damaged, you would have to purchase a new copy.

If you should lose or damage the working copy, you can always use the original program diskette to make another working copy.

2. The working copy of Home Mortgage Calculator is made self-loading. This means that if the working copy of Home Mortgage Calculator is placed in drive A of your computer and the computer is turned on, Home Mortgage Calculator will automatically load and start running by itself.

To do this, your computer's operating system will have to be put on the working copy of Home Mortgage Calculator. This is done automatically in the preparation process.

To make your working copy, be sure you have the formatted diskette, described earlier, ready to go.

Depending on whether you have a one-disk drive, two-disk drive, or hard disk system, follow the appropriate instructions to make your working copy of the original program diskette. *(To save space, only the two-drive system process is explained in this manual.—Ed.)*

If you encounter any error messages when making the working copy, follow the instructions given to you earlier in the introduction to this manual.

## Making Your Working Copy with a Two-Disk Drive System

Step 1   Insert your DOS diskette into drive A of your computer. Turn the computer on.

Step 2   After several seconds (the amount of time depends on how much memory your computer has) DOS will ask for today's date and the current time. Enter the correct information. After this is entered, you should see the system prompt: a› displayed on your video display screen.

Step 3   Leaving the DOS diskette in drive A, insert the original program diskette in drive B.

Step 4   Now type in the following command after the system prompt: B:PREPARE and then press the: ENTER key. After about four seconds the following message is displayed:
The first preparatory step is complete. Proceed with the next step.

Step 5   Now remove the original program diskette from drive B and replace it with the blank formatted diskette.

Step 6   Now press the: ENTER key. After about six seconds, the following message is displayed:
The second preparatory step is complete. Proceed with the next step.

Step 7   Now remove the DOS diskette from drive A and replace it with the original program diskette.

Step 8   Now press the: ENTER key. After about ten seconds, the following message is displayed:
The preparation process is now complete.
A›

You have completed the preparation process and are almost ready to begin the tutorial. Before you do, though, be sure you store the original program diskette in a safe location. Also don't forget to label the working copy of Home Mortgage Calculator.

You may repeat the preparation process any time you need to make additional copies of Home Mortgage Calculator for your own use.

**Printer Setup**

Once you have prepared your working copy of Home Mortgage Calculator, the second preparatory step is to tell Home Mortgage Calculator what printer, if any, you have connected to your computer. This is done because some printers work differently from others.

Home Mortgage Calculator will work without your taking this step, but you will not be able to print the calculator screen or any of the comparison tables displayed on the video display screen.

Step 1   If you have not turned your computer off since completing the working copy, the DOS system prompt should be displayed on the screen: A›. If you have turned off the computer since making the working copy, you will have to restart the computer using the DOS diskette and reenter the date and time.

Step 2   Insert the working copy of Home Mortgage Calculator in drive A.

Step 3   Type the command: PRINTER and press the ENTER key. This step loads the "printer" program that is used to set up Home Mortgage Calculator for your printer. After about four seconds, the following screen is displayed:
Printer Setup Program
1) Parallel Printer
2) Serial Printer
3) No Printer
Enter the appropriate number corresponding to the printer type you have installed to your computer.

Step 4   After you enter a number, the screen will clear and the system prompt will appear. Home Mortgage Calculator is now ready for use with a printer.

Should you ever change printers, you can run the printer setup program any time you want, to let Home Mortgage Calculator know of the change.

# Tutorial: Using Home Mortgage Calculator

## Introduction

This section of Home Mortgage Calculator's manual is the most important. Step by step, you will learn how to use all of Home Mortgage Calculator's features.

The tutorial will take about one-half hour to complete and it is recommended that you try to complete it all at one sitting. Home Mortgage Calculator is easier to learn this way.

The tutorial is divided into four sections. They are:

1. Loading Home Mortgage Calculator
2. Using the Calculator Screen
3. Displaying and Printing Comparison Tables
4. Exiting Home Mortgage Calculator

Each section is itself divided into four parts. They are:

1. A description of the operation
2. Examples for you to try
3. Practical exercises and their answers. (Used where applicable)
4. Summary

While completing the tutorial, don't be afraid to experiment. You can't hurt or damage the program or computer. If you ever get into a situation you don't know how to get out of, just restart the program using your computer system's reset.

## Loading Home Mortgage Calculator

Before you can use Home Mortgage Calculator, it must be loaded into your computer. There are two ways to load Home Mortgage Calculator. The first

method assumes that your computer is off and the second method assumes that your computer is already on and the system prompt is displayed.

## Loading Home Mortgage Calculator When Your Computer Is Off

Step 1    Insert the working copy of Home Mortgage Calculator into drive A. Turn your computer on. After several seconds your computer will automatically load the DOS and Home Mortgage Calculator and automatically start the program. The date and time usually requested by the DOS are bypassed as they serve no function in the program.

The first display on your video display screen will be the title and copyright screen. See Figure 2. It appears for six seconds and then is replaced by the Home Mortgage Calculator calculator screen. See Figure 3.

## Loading Home Mortgage Calculator When Your Computer Is Already On

The second method assumes that your computer is already on and the DOS has been loaded and the system prompt: A> is displayed on your screen. You might use method #2 instead of method #1 if you have completed some other task on your computer and you now want to use Home Mortgage Calculator. This way you don't have to turn your computer off and then on again or do a system reset.

Step 1    Insert the working copy of Home Mortgage Calculator in drive A.

---

Step 2    Now type the command: HMC and press the: ENTER key. After about five seconds, Home Mortgage Calculator loads and automatically begins running. You will see the title and copyright screen (Figure 2), and after six seconds, the Home Mortgage Calculator calculator screen will be displayed (Figure 3).

---

HMC is the name of the program on the Home Mortgage Calculator working copy diskette that starts the program. It may be used at any time to start the program from DOS.

## Summary

•    There are two ways to start Home Mortgage Calculator:
The first assumes that your computer is off. Place the working copy into drive A and turn your computer on. After several seconds, the program will begin.
The second assumes that your computer is on. Place the working copy into drive A and enter the command HMC. After several seconds, the program will begin.

## Using the Calculator Screen

As was discussed in the introduction, Home Mortgage Calculator is designed to calculate any one of the following financing terms:

- Purchase Price
- Percentage Down Payment
- Loan Term
- Annual Interest Rate
- Monthly Payment

All you have to do is to supply any four of the five financing terms and Home Mortgage Calculator calculates the remaining financing term. This way, you can experiment with different combinations of financing terms.

As you learned in the previous section, after the program is loaded and the title screen appears for a short time, the calculator screen appears. The calculator screen is divided into two windows: the calculator window and the comparison window.

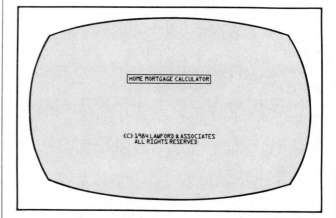

**Figure 2.** *Title and Copyright Screen*

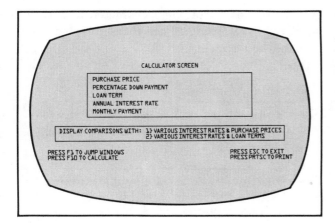

Figure 3. *Calculator Screen*

---

## The Calculator Screen
If the calculator screen is not now displayed on your computer's video display, load the program. You should see the screen shown in Figure 4.

Before you can use Home Mortgage Calculator, you must learn how to move about the calculator screen.

## The Cursor
Look at the calculator screen carefully. You should see a dark flashing dash in the box after the "Purchase Price" financing term. This is the cursor. Whenever you want to enter a financing term, you must first move the cursor to the box corresponding to the financing term.

Moving the Cursor with the TAB (—›, ‹— ) key.

To move the cursor from one box to another

you must press the TAB key. Each press of the TAB key jumps the cursor from one box to the one below it.

Step 1   Press the: TAB key once to see it jump to the box below it.

---

Step 2   Try pressing the TAB key several more times for practice.

---

Did you notice that when the cursor jumped to the last box in the calculator window, the next press of the TAB key jumped the cursor back up to the first box, corresponding to Purchase Price?

When the cursor gets to the last box, it has no place to go but to the top box.

Using the SHIFT and TAB keys

You may not always want the cursor to jump down to the next box. If you want the cursor to jump to the previous box, press the SHIFT key along with TAB key. This will cause the cursor to jump to the previous box.

Step 1   Press the: SHIFT key and the: TAB key at the same time. The cursor jumps up one box.

---

Step 2   Press the SHIFT and TAB key combination several more times for practice.

---

As happened before, when you press the SHIFT and TAB key combination and the cursor is at the top box, the cursor will jump to the bottom box as it has no other place to go.

**Entering Financing Terms in the
Calculator Window**

Step 1   Use the TAB key to move the
         cursor to Purchase Price.

_____

Step 2   Enter the number: 65000 just as
         you see it. As you enter each
         number, you see that a dollar sign
         is automatically placed at the left of
         the value, that a comma is
         automatically inserted at the
         proper location in the value, and
         that a decimal point and two zeros
         are placed to the right of the
         number. The number should look
         like this: $65,000.00 on the screen
         after you have finished entering it.

_____

The automatic dollar sign, comma, decimal
point, and zeros are a feature of Home
Mortgage Calculator that reduces the
amount of keying you have to do. If you
enter a number that requires decimal
numbers, all you have to do is enter the
number with the decimal point. When you
are entering the annual interest rate, a
percent sign is automatically displayed.

**Correcting Errors**
Should you make a mistake when you enter
a financing term, there are two ways to
correct the error.

**Method #1**
If you make an error and catch it
immediately, you can correct it by pressing
the ←— (backspace) key. Pressing the ←— key
erases the character you just entered. Pressing

it again erases the previous character, and so on
until you have erased all the characters and the
variable box is empty.

Step 1   Press the ←— once. The display should
         change from: $65,000.00 to: $6,500.00

_____

Step 2   Go ahead and press the ←— key four
         more times until the variable box is
         empty.

_____

Step 3   Now enter the following number
         into the same variable box:
         65000.25
         As was mentioned before, enter the
         numbers and decimal point exactly
         as pictured above. When you are
         done, it should appear like this:
         $65,000.25 on the screen.

_____

**Method #2**
The second way to correct errors is to use
the cursor control keys to move the cursor
under the character(s) that need to be
changed and then to type over the error(s).

Step 1   Let's say that instead of $65,000.25,
         you meant to enter $65,000.40. To
         correct this error, use the left
         cursor control key to position the
         cursor under the "2".

_____

Step 2   Now press the: 4 key. The incorrect
         "2" is now replaced with the correct
         "4", and the cursor is now located
         under the "5".

_____

Step 3   Now press the: 0 key. The incorrect
         "5" is replaced with the correct "0".

Experiment with this method of correction using numbers you make up. Practice until you feel comfortable with this correction method.

## Making Your First Calculation:
## Example #1

Step 1   Enter the following numbers in the calculator window:

| | |
|---|---|
| Purchase Price | 65000 |
| Percentage Down Payment | 10 |
| Loan Term | 20 |
| Annual Interest Rate | 12 |

If you make any mistakes, use the error correction methods you learned above.

You have entered four of the five necessary variables needed to make a calculation. Since you are calculating the monthly mortgage amount, you leave it blank.

Step 2   To solve for the monthly mortgage amount, press the F10 key. Instantly, the result, $644.14, is displayed in the calculator window. See Figure 5.

Whenever you solve for any of the financing terms, you always follow the same procedure. You enter four of the five financing terms and leave the fifth one empty. Pressing the F10 key will then solve for the missing variable.

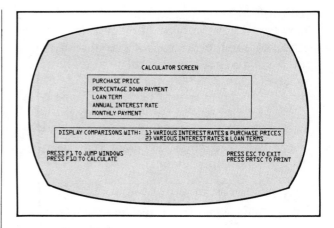

**Figure 4.** *Calculator Screen*

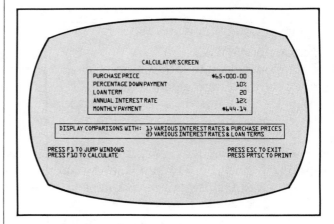

**Figure 5.** *Completed Calculation*

## Example #2

Now try the same type of calculation, but with one small change. Let's assume that you want to find the monthly payment of a house costing $70,000 instead of $65,000.

Step 1    If the cursor is not already in the Monthly Payment box, use the TAB key to move it there. Use the backspace key to clear the box of the previous entry.

---

Step 2    Use the TAB key to move the cursor to the Purchase Price box and change the current entry to $70,000.

---

Step 3    Press the F10 key and the new answer, $693.68, is immediately displayed in the Monthly Payment box.

---

## Example #3

Let's now calculate a purchase price given a monthly mortgage amount of $683.77.

Step 1    Clear out the Purchase Price box, and into the Monthly Payment box enter: 683.77

---

Step 2    Press the F10 key, and the answer, $69,000.00, will be displayed in the Purchase Price box.

---

## More Practice

For practice, below are some combinations of financing terms with an unknown that you can solve for. The correct answer is included so you can check your practice.

## Exercise #1

Purchase Price
Percentage Down Payment . . . . . . . .      20
Loan Term . . . . . . . . . . . . . . . . . . . . .      30
Annual Interest Rate . . . . . . . . . . . . .   12.71
Monthly Payment . . . . . . . . . . . . . . . 650.15

Answer: Purchase Price is $75,000.

## Exercise #2

Purchase Price . . . . . . . . . . . . . . . . . .150,000
Percentage Down Payment
Loan Term . . . . . . . . . . . . . . . . . . . . .      25
Annual Interest Rate . . . . . . . . . . . . .   10.75
Monthly Payment . . . . . . . . . . . . . . .1,298.83

Answer: Percentage Down Payment is 10%.

## Exercise #3

Purchase Price . . . . . . . . . . . . . . . . . . 65,000
Percentage Down Payment . . . . . . . . .      10
Loan Term
Annual Interest Rate . . . . . . . . . . . . .   12.75
Monthly Payment . . . . . . . . . . . . . . . 628.99

Answer: Loan Term is 35 years.

## Exercise #4

Purchase Price . . . . . . . . . . . . . . . . . . 66,000
Percentage Down Payment . . . . . . . . .      10
Loan Term . . . . . . . . . . . . . . . . . . . . .      20
Annual Interest Rate
Monthly Payment . . . . . . . . . . . . . . . 664.43

Answer: Annual Interest Rate is 12.25%.

## Exercise #5

Purchase Price . . . . . . . . . . . . . . . . . . 72,900
Percentage Down Payment . . . . . . . . .       3

Loan Term . . . . . . . . . . . . . . . . . . . . . . . . . 30
Annual Interest Rate . . . . . . . . . . . . . . 12.9
Monthly Payment

Answer: Monthly Payment is $776.70.

## Printing the Calculator Screen
Should you ever want a printed copy of the calculator screen, you need only to press the PRTSC key with the printer on and loaded with paper. If you have a printer, try this example.

Step 1  Make sure you have a completed calculation in the calculator window.

Step 2  Make sure your printer is on and the paper is positioned properly.

Step 3  Press the: PRTSC key. The printer should immediately print a copy of the calculator screen on your paper.

## Summary
•   You must supply four out of the five financing terms in the calculator window. The remaining financing term is solved for.
•   Use the TAB key to jump the cursor to the next variable box.
•   Use the SHIFT and TAB key (pressed at the same time) to jump the cursor to the previous variable box.
•   Use the BACKSPACE or cursor control keys to correct your mistakes.
•   Use the F10 key to calculate the missing variable.
•   Use the PRTSC key to print the calculator screen.

## Displaying and Printing Comparison Tables

While the figures calculated above are useful, it is often an advantage to see these financial terms in a comparison table so that you can see the whole financial picture at once. Home Mortgage Calculator allows you to examine two different types of comparison tables.

## To Begin With
At the bottom of the calculator screen (assuming you are still in front of your computer) is the comparison window. *Before you can display any comparison table, you must do two things:*
1. You must have the top four financing terms entered in the calculator window. Home Mortgage Calculator uses these values to calculate the comparison tables. If they do not have values and you tell Home Mortgage Calculator to display a table, you will receive an error message on the screen.
2. You must move the cursor to the comparison window from the calculator window.

## Displaying Your First Table—Example #1
In this example you will display a comparison table of monthly payments at various interest rates and purchase prices.

Step 1  For this example, reenter (if they are not already there) the financing terms in the calculator window you used the first time you made a calculation. They are:
Purchase Price                  65000
Percentage Down Payment          10

Loan Term                                    20
Annual Interest Rate                         12
As was mentioned before, the first four of the five financing terms must have values.

Step 2    Next you must move the cursor to the comparison window from the calculator window. Press the: F1 key to do this. Each time you press the F1 key, the cursor jumps from one window to the other.

Step 3    Now enter a: 1 in the box where the cursor is located in the comparison window. This selects the first comparison option: "Various Interest Rates & Purchase Prices." The screen should look like the one in Figure 6.

Step 4    Now press the: ENTER key. Instantly, Home Mortgage Calculator displays the comparison table. See Figure 7.

This table uses the loan term you entered in the calculator window and gives you the monthly payments at various combinations of interest rates and purchase prices. Home Mortgage Calculator automatically increments the interest rate and purchase price at intervals starting from the amounts you entered in the calculator window.

The table allows you to see how different interest rates and purchase prices affect the monthly mortgage payment. After examining the table, press the ESC key to return to the main menu. Always press the ESC key to return to the calculator screen from the comparison table.

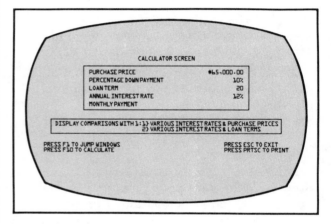

**Figure 6.** *Getting Ready to Display Comparison Screen*

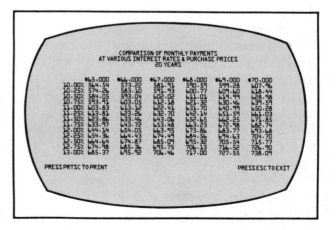

**Figure 7.** *Variable Interest Rates & Purchase Prices*

## Example #2
Displaying the second table, showing the monthly payments at various interest rates and loan terms, using the same financing terms used before, is very similar to the previous example.

Step 1   You should be at the comparison window and the cursor should be flashing in the small box. Enter a: 2 in the box. The "2" will replace the "1" already in the box.

Step 2   Press the: ENTER key and the table shown in Figure 8 will be displayed.

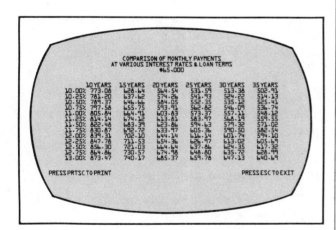

**Figure 8.** *Variable Interest Rates & Loan Terms*

This table uses the purchase price you entered in the calculator window. It allows you to see how different interest rates and loan terms affect the monthly mortgage payment. Home Mortgage Calculator

increments the interest rate and loan terms as in the previous example. After examining the table, press the ESC key to return to the main menu.

## How to Get Different Comparisons
To see different comparison tables, all you have to do is to change the financing terms found in the calculator window and redisplay the table.

## More Practice
Experiment now, changing the variables and displaying comparison tables until you feel comfortable with this feature.

## Printing Tables
If you have a printer, you can print any table just as you printed the calculator screen before

Step 1   You must first have a table displayed on the screen.

Step 2   Be sure your printer is on and the paper is positioned properly.

Step 3   Press the: PRTSC key and the table will be printed. If you plan ahead and adjust the paper to start from the top of the sheet, you can print up to three different tables on an 8½x11-inch sheet of paper, if you don't advance the paper between each table you print.

# Reference Section

## Summary

• Before a table can be displayed, the top four financing terms must have entries in the calculator window.
• Choose the type of table by entering either a "1" or "2" in the comparison box on the calculator screen and press ENTER.
• You can create different tables by changing any of the four financing terms in the calculator window. Any change of the financing terms creates a completely new table.
• Press the PRTSC key to print a table.

## Exiting Home Mortgage Calculator

You may exit Home Mortgage Calculator any time you like.

Step 1   You must have the calculator screen displayed on the video display terminal.

Step 2   Press the: ESC key. Immediately you are returned to your computer's operating system, and the system prompt: A› is displayed on the screen.

## Introduction

This reference section provides an easy way for you to look up information about the use of Home Mortgage Calculator. If you didn't understand some concept after going through the tutorial, or if you have forgotten something because you have not used Home Mortgage Calculator in some time, you will find the answers to all your questions in this section.

## How to Use the Reference Section

The reference section is divided into four sections. They are:

1. Loading Home Mortgage Calculator
2. Using the Calculator Screen
3. Displaying and Printing Comparison Tables
4. Exiting Home Mortgage Calculator

Each of these sections is divided into two parts. They are:

1. Purpose of section
2. Description of use

Whenever you have any questions about using any part of Home Mortgage Calculator, first turn to the relevant section. If you are not sure which section to refer to, read the "Purpose" to aid your search.

Once you have the appropriate section, locate the information you need by examining the headings.

# Loading Home Mortgage Calculator

**Purpose:**
How to load Home Mortgage Calculator.

There are two different ways to load Home Mortgage Calculator into your computer. They are:

**Computer is off**
If your computer is off, insert the working copy of Home Mortgage Calculator into disk drive A and turn your computer on. After a few seconds, the title and copyright screen will be displayed. After six more seconds, the calculator screen is displayed and you are ready to proceed with the program.

**Computer is on**
If your computer is on and the system prompt is displayed, insert the working copy of Home Mortgage Calculator into disk drive A. Then enter the command "HMC" and press ENTER. After a few seconds, the title and copyright screen will be displayed. After six more seconds, the calculator screen will be displayed and you are ready to proceed with the program.

You may use the command "HMC" any time you want to load Home Mortgage Calculator if the system prompt is displayed on the video display terminal and the working copy is in disk drive A.

# Using the Calculator Screen

**Purpose:**
How to use Home Mortage Calculator to calculate any of the following variables: Purchase Price, Percentage Down Payment, Loan Term, Annual Interest Rate, or Monthly Payment.

The calculator screen is divided into two windows: the calculator window and the comparison window. The calculator window allows you to enter financing terms, perform calculations, and displays results. All you have to do is to supply four of the five variables and press the F10 (CALCULATE) key. The answer is instantly displayed.

**How to Solve For:**

**Purchase Price** Enter appropriate values in the Percentage Down Payment, Loan Term, Annual Interest Rate, and Monthly Payment boxes. Be sure that the Purchase Price box is empty. Press the F10 key. The answer is instantly displayed.

**Percentage Down Payment** Enter appropriate values in the Purchase Price, Loan Term, Annual Interest Rate, and Monthly Payment boxes. Be sure that the Percentage Down Payment box is empty. Press the F10 key. The answer is instantly displayed.

**Loan Term** Enter appropriate values in the Purchase Price, Percentage Down Payment, Annual Interest Rate, and Monthly Payment boxes. Be sure that the Loan Term box is empty. Press the F10 key. The answer is instantly displayed.

# Displaying and Printing Comparison Tables

**Annual Interest Rate** Enter appropriate values in the Purchase Price, Percentage Down Payment, Loan Term, and Monthly Payment boxes. Be sure that the Annual Interest Rate box is empty. Press the F10 key. The answer is instantly displayed.

**Monthly Payment** Enter appropriate values in the Purchase Price, Percentage Down Payment, Loan Term, and Annual Interest Rate boxes. Be sure that the Monthly Payment box is empty. Press the F10 key. The answer is instantly displayed.

**Purpose:**
How to display and print two different types of comparison tables: (1) Compare monthly payments given various interest rates and purchase prices; and (2) Compare monthly payments given various interest rates and loan terms.

Before either comparison table can be displayed, the first four of the five financing terms—Purchase Price, Percentage Down Payment, Loan Term, and Annual Interest Rate—must be entered in the calculator window.

Given the financing terms you entered, Home Mortgage Calculator displays two different comparison tables. To see variations of these two tables, one or more of the financing terms entered must be changed. This causes different tables to be displayed.

**How to Display and Print:**

**Comparison Table #1** After you have entered the first four financing terms into the calculator window, enter a "1" in the box in the comparison window and press ENTER. Comparison table #1 is instantly displayed. Press the PRTSC key if you want to print the table, or press the ESC key to return to the calculator screen.

**Comparison Table #2** After you have entered the first four financing terms into the calculator window, enter a "2" in the box in the comparison window and press ENTER. Comparison table #2 is instantly displayed. Press the PRTSC key if you want to print the table, or press the ESC key to return to the calculator screen.

# Exiting Home Mortgage Calculator

**Purpose:**
How to exit the Home Mortgage Calculator program.

You may exit the Home Mortgage Calculator program at any time. All you have to do is press the ESC key when the calculator screen is displayed. You will immediately be returned to the computer's operating system, and the system prompt will be displayed on the screen.

# Appendix A: Error Messages *(Abbreviated list—Ed.)*

When any of these error messages appear on your screen while you are using Home Mortgage Calculator, find the message in the following list and take the appropriate corrective action. These error messages are given by your computer, not by Home Mortgage Calculator.

### Disk Media Error

**Cause:** There are two possible causes: (1) a bad diskette is being used for the working copy; or (2) there is a computer hardware malfunction. This error occurs when you try to load Home Mortgage Calculator.

**Action #1** First try making a new working copy on the same floppy diskette. If you retry loading the program and you still get the same error, discard the old diskette and make a working copy on a new diskette. Load Home Mortgage Calculator and proceed as usual.

**Action #2** If solution #1 does not work, then you may have a computer hardware problem. See your computer dealer for assistance.

### Disk Not Ready

**Cause:** There are two possible causes: (1) the working copy is not in disk drive A; or (2) the disk drive door is not closed. This error occurs when you try to load Home Mortgage Calculator.

**Action #1** Check to see that the working

# Glossary

copy of Home Mortgage Calculator is in disk drive A. Load Home Mortgage Calculator as usual.

**Action #2** Check to see that the disk drive door is closed properly. Load Home Mortgage Calculator as usual.

**Annual Interest Rate.** The amount of the annual interest rate (or annual percentage rate) charged by a lending institution for a home mortgage loan.

**Box.** Refers to a rectangular box of light on the screen. All information entered into Home Mortgage Calculator is entered in these boxes.

**Calculator Screen.** This is the heart of Home Mortgage Calculator. It is made up of the calculator window and the comparison window.

**Calculator Window.** The top window of the calculator screen, where financing terms are entered, calculations occur, and results are displayed.

**Comparison Table.** A table of possible monthly mortgage payments based on various combinations of financing terms.

**Comparison Window.** The bottom window of the calculator screen, where you choose what type of comparison table you want displayed.

**Copy Protected.** A program diskette that is copy protected cannot be copied by means of the conventional DOS copy program. The Home Mortgage Calculator program diskette is not copy protected and thus can be copied with the DOS copy program.

**Cursor.** This is the flashing dash seen on the calculating screen. Whenever something is entered on the screen, it is placed at the location of the cursor.

**Disk Operating System (DOS).** A program that handles the internal operations of a computer. It must be loaded in the computer when the machine is first turned on.

**Formatted.** A floppy diskette that is formatted has been specially prepared for use by a computer. A special DOS program, called the FORMAT program, is used to prepare the diskette.

**Loan Term.** The total number of years the mortgage will be financed by the lending institution. For example: 20 years, 30 years.

**Monthly Payment.** The monthly payment that is made to the lending institution for the term of the mortgage loan. This includes both interest and principal amounts.

**Percentage Down Payment.** The percentage of the purchase price that is to be the down payment for the mortgage loan. For example: 10 percent, 15 percent.

**Program.** A set of instructions that tell a computer what to do. Home Mortgage Calculator is a program.

**Program Diskette.** This is the original floppy diskette you get when you purchase Home Mortgage Calculator. It contains the various programs that make up Home Mortgage Calculator. The program diskette should not be employed in everyday use but, once copied, it should be stored in a safe location.

**Purchase Price.** The negotiated price of the house that is being considered for purchase; the price you will be paying the seller for the house.

**Screen.** The information displayed on your video display monitor at any point in time.

**System Prompt.** The symbol given by the DOS that tells the user that the DOS is available for a command.

**System Reset.** Usually a keystroke (or series of keystrokes) that restarts a computer without your turning it off.

**Video Display Terminal.** The physical hardware where information is displayed by a computer on a TV-like screen.

**Working Copy.** This is the copy of the original program diskette of Home Mortgage Calculator that you make for everyday use.

# Home Mortgage Calculator User Manual

**Common Keyboard Commands**

| | |
|---|---|
| F1 | **JUMP key.** Used to jump the cursor from one window on the calculator screen to the other. |
| F10 | **CALCULATE key.** Used to calculate the unknown financing term. |
| ESC | **ESCAPE key (EXIT key).** Used to return to the calculator screen from the comparison table. Also, if you press ESC while at the calculator screen, you will exit the program and return to the operating system of your computer. |
| PRTSC | **PRINT SCREEN key.** Used to print either the calculator screen or the comparison tables. |
| ENTER | **ENTER key.** Used to cause the computer to act on your previously entered command. |
| $\longrightarrow$ | **TAB key.** Used to move from one financing term to another. Each time you press it, the cursor will jump to the next term. Pressing the shift key and the tab key at the same time moves the cursor to the previous financing term. |
| $\longleftarrow$ | **BACKSPACE key.** Used to correct errors. It moves the cursor one space back and removes any character in that space. |

**Lawford & Associates**

| | |
|---|---|
| 4 | **Cursor Control keys.** Used |
| ‹ | to correct keyboard entries. |
| 6 | Moves the cursor left or |
| —› | right, one character at a |
| | time, without erasing any |
| | characters. |

# Loading Home Mortgage Calculator

When the computer is off:

Insert the working copy of Home Mortgage Calculator into disk drive A and turn your computer on. After several seconds, you are ready to proceed with the program.

When the computer is on:

Insert the working copy of Home Mortgage Calculator into disk drive A. Then enter the command "HMC" after the system prompt and press ENTER. After several seconds, you are ready to proceed with the program.

# Using the Calculator Screen

Enter four out of the five variables into the calculator window and press the F10 (CALCULATE key). The unknown variable will be instantly displayed.

The variables you have available include the home purchase price, percentage down payment, loan term, annual interest rate, and monthly down payment.

# Displaying and Printing Comparison Tables

How to display the comparison of monthly payments given various interest rates and purchase prices:

After you have entered the first four financing terms into the calculator window, enter a "1" in the box in the comparison window and press ENTER. The table is instantly displayed.

How to display the comparison of monthly payments given various interest rates and loan terms:

After you have entered the first four financing terms into the calculator window, enter a "2" in the box in the comparison window and press ENTER. The table is instantly displayed.

# Exiting Home Mortgage Calculator

Pressing the ESC key when at the calculator window will return you to the computer's operating system.

# 10. Illustrating Your Manual

A magazine without any pictures or illustrations would be boring. The long columns of prose would go on and on without a break until an article happened to end. The monotony would probably keep most readers from finishing the magazine. They might skip around trying to find interesting tidbits, but no more.

Software user manuals, like magazines, need illustrations to break up the prose into easily read blocks of text and to make reading more interesting. Manual illustrations such as screen and report facsimiles, tables and diagrams, and drawings of computer equipment increase the effectiveness of manuals by visually expressing exactly what your words say. They show readers at a glance what you mean and they often reduce the number of words required to make a point. A manual that is interesting to read also communicates more efficiently to the reader.

**Communicating with Illustrations**

As with prose, there are guidelines to follow when you use illustrations to enhance communication. They are:

1. Whereas words are better to tell the reader *how* to perform a task, to explain *why* it is done, and even to suggest *when* to carry it out, illustrations are better for showing *what* to do and *where* to do it. Try to make words and illustrations work together to bring about the best possible communication, each fulfilling its respective role.

2. Do not substitute illustrations where words are necessary. Lazy writers often try to use a series of diagrams to show step-by-step procedures without explanatory text. Without exception, text and illustrations must complement each other.

3. While reading your text, the reader should be directed to relevant illustrations at the place in the text where the illustrations will amplify and complement what is being discussed. If you wait until later to make a reference to an illustration, or if you neglect to make any reference at all, the reader is forced to reread previous text to discover the meaning of the illustration when he gets to it.

4. Place each illustration in the body of your text as soon as possible *after* the reference to it is made. Although this is not always easy to do, it saves the reader from flipping back or forth several pages to find the illustration. Closely placed text and illustrations not only are a convenience to the reader, they contribute to successful communication, as the reader does not have to break his train of thought looking for the illustration.

**5.** With few exceptions, illustrations should be numbered and captioned. Numbering makes it easier to refer to an illustration from the text. (See Figure 10-1.) Captions explain the illustration and reinforce what was discussed in the text. Also, when a reader refers to the manual at a later time, captioned illustrations save him from having to search through the text to find something out about the illustration. Be consistent in your numbering system.

**Figure 10-1**
*Video screen with grid for type*

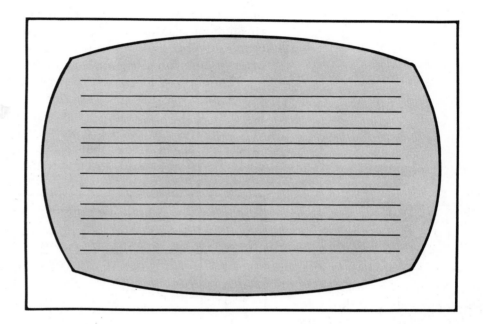

**6.** Each illustration should convey only one idea. Trying to make illustrations do double duty will only confuse the reader.
**7.** Illustrations should not be cluttered with detail but done simply so that the idea they are to convey is not masked by anything else.

## Types of Illustrations

Likenesses of screens and reports, tables and diagrams, and drawings of computer hardware are some of the more common illustrations used in software user manuals. Each has its place in showing exactly what you mean. Which type of illustration will best complement your text is usually obvious, and the choice should present no problem. Illustrating screens, tables of control codes, and drawings of switch settings are self-evident. What might be more difficult for you to decide are the trade-offs in the quality of the illustrations. Usually, there are several ways you can produce an illustration, each with advantages and disadvantages. Your choice will often depend on what the illustrations are intended to communicate.

Here is a look at some of the most common illustrations used in manuals and a discussion of the trade-offs involved.

### Screens and Reports

Of all the illustrations found in manuals, these are the most common. Screens, of course, are likenesses of displays on video display screens and are used to show the user what is happening on the screen at any given time. Reports, on the other hand, are the printed hard copy generated by a printer attached to the computer.

In the manual's tutorial the reader must be told step by step what to do. Because the video display screen is the way a microcomputer communicates with the user, it must be depicted often throughout the tutorial, showing what menus, error messages, and responses look like. When portraying these screens in the tutorial, or anywhere in the manual, you have several options.

The easiest method is to draw a facsimile of a video display screen and type the screen's text using a typewriter or word processor. This is quick and inexpensive and is often satisfactory to readers. Of course a drawing of a screen can never quite duplicate what is actually on the screen, but most readers can take the psychological leap and understand your intentions. (See Figure 10-2.)

**Figure 10-2**

*While this likeness of a video display screen is not an entirely accurate representation of what the user sees on his computer, in most cases he will get the point of what you are trying to illustrate.*

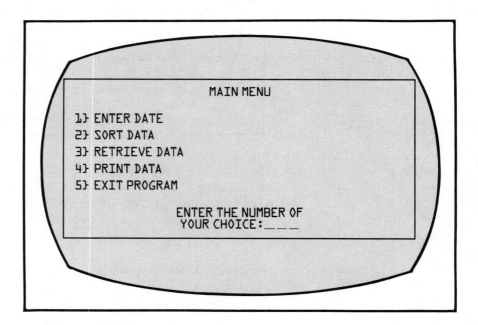

```
                    MAIN MENU

        1} ENTER DATE
        2} SORT DATA
        3} RETRIEVE DATA
        4} PRINT DATA
        5} EXIT PROGRAM


               ENTER THE NUMBER OF
               YOUR CHOICE:____
```

This simple method of screen depiction works best when the screens are simple and contain text and perhaps some numeric information. This is so because the size of the type made by typewriters and printers is relatively large compared with the size of the screen that can be drawn, and you cannot get as much text and numbers on the drawing as can be shown on a real video display terminal. One way to overcome this problem is to typeset the characters used in the screen depiction. Typesetting allows you to vary the size of type so that you can come closer to representing the screen on a video display terminal. However, your screen illustration will not

Writing Software User Manuals

be 100 percent realistic or be able to show complex screens.

If you want to show illustrations of screens that are exactly the way they are depicted on a video display terminal, photography is the best choice. Photographs of the screen render the screen accurately so readers will know exactly what to expect and will not be likely to misinterpret anything. Also, photographs faultlessly portray complicated screens like those found on graphics and spreadsheet programs.

Although photographs are the ideal choice when depicting screens, they are expensive, both to photograph and to print. Usually the best trade-off to make, depending on your budget, is to use a combination of drawings with text and photographs. Use the drawings for simple screen responses, ones that will not confuse the reader, and use photographs of screens that could cause confusion if they were not accurately portrayed.

On a very low-budget manual you may not be able to use photographs. In this case, you might consider making the screen drawings as large as possible, even a whole page, to include all the information as accurately as possible.

Illustrations of reports are easier to produce than those of screens. The easiest and least expensive method is just to print the report as you would normally on your printer and use it as a full-page illustration. Printers have special ways of copying and reproducing your printouts. They can be reduced to almost any size to fit the needs of your manual. You will want to add a figure number to it and a caption, but that can be done by typing or typesetting the information on a piece of paper and pasting it at the bottom of the report.

Typesetting an entire report is expensive and will not produce a realistic depiction of the report; it should be avoided.

**Tables and Diagrams**
This is a general category, lumping together everything that is not a screen, report, or hardware drawing. In writing the manual, you may find it useful to list important and lengthy information into tables for easy use, such as a list of program variables with their respective uses. You may also want to draw a diagram of a flowchart showing the accounting cycle of a general ledger program. The illustrations can be as varied as necessary to enhance your text. (See Figure 10-3.)

Most tables can be created on a typewriter or word processor. Line up the information in table form and use the underline and hyphen keys to mark divisions of material. If you are careful, they can be as clear as a typeset table, although they might not look as neat.

Diagrams might be more difficult to do on a typewriter or word processor, and you may require typesetting or a professional artist to create them neatly and accurately. Your diagram needs and publishing budget determine what you can do.

**Figure 10-3**
*This table is easy to create with either a typewriter or word processing software. For extra neatness, it can be typeset if you desire.*

---

**Which Printers Work with Electronic Encyclopedia**

| Brand | | Parallel Connection | | Serial Connection |
|---|---|---|---|---|
| WorkHorse 100 | : | Yes | : | Yes |
| SpeedWhiz 200 | : | Yes | : | No |
| HiTech Z150 | : | Yes | : | Yes |
| FancyWriter | : | No | : | Yes |
| Run Writer 500 | : | Yes | : | Yes |
| Sprinter 5000 | : | No | : | No |
| BX-200 | : | No | : | No |

---

**Drawings**

Drawings are normally used to illustrate computer equipment and procedures relating to it. For example, you might want to illustrate, step by step, how to insert a diskette into a disk drive and turn the computer on. You could do this by showing a series of illustrations that correspond to the procedures you describe in your text.

In most cases, drawings are a luxury that manual makers cannot afford. Unless you are a professional artist or drafter, you will have to hire a freelance artist. This is both expensive and time-consuming. Fortunately, such drawings are not mandatory in software manuals. They do contribute to clarity, but careful writing can usually eliminate the need for them. When you are making the decision whether or not to go with drawings, think first about your audience. The more inexperienced the potential reader, the greater the need for illustrations, especially drawings. Do not make this decision on cost alone.

**How to Create Illustrations**

The thought of creating illustrations can make some manual writers nervous. This should not be so. While you may not be an artist, you can do many of the illustrations yourself. If you can't, you can learn how to work with professional illustrators to get the illustrations you need. The following section tells you how to create many common illustrations and how to find and work with professionals if need be.

Writing Software User Manuals

## Planning

Illustrations for the manual should be planned at the same time as the text. In the earliest stages of planning the manual, you should have an idea of what your budget is and the type of illustrations you will be using. (See Chapters 4 and 5.) Knowing your limitations at this point will smooth the later stages of creating the manual. Later, in the outlining stage, specific illustrations should be decided on and fitted in with the text. This system ensures that the actual writing and illustration stage will proceed with few problems; also, if you are going to hire professionals, you can plan so their work will be done in plenty of time.

## Screens

The easiest way to illustrate a screen is first to use a typewriter or word processor to type the contents of the screen on a sheet of paper, located on the paper where you want the screen located. Then, using a template of the screen (cardboard makes great templates; it can be cut into the shape of a video display screen), draw the outline of a screen around the contents. Use different size templates to show different amounts of text. This way your illustration gives the illusion of being a screen from a video display terminal. Granted, it is not a neat or accurate representation, but it can work well in manuals.

Another way to create illustrations of screens is to have a printer create templates of various sizes and have the contents of the screens typeset. This method requires careful planning on your part, and you should go ahead and follow the previously described template procedure when you write the manual. After it is written and ready to be typeset, the screens will be redone by the printer to match your specifications. The rough screens will guide the printer's work.

The third and most accurate way to represent screens is through photography. The photography can be done by yourself or by a professional photographer. If you take the screen photographs yourself, follow these guidelines to get the best results:

1. *Equipment.* You will need a 35mm single-lens reflex camera with manual exposure capability, a 100mm or longer telephoto lens, and a tripod.

2. *Film.* Almost any 35mm film works, but Tri-X with a film speed (ASA/ISO) of 400 is suggested. Its high speed reduces the length of the exposure, preventing the possibility that the camera will be shaken during the exposure and the photograph will become blurred.

3. *Setup.* Position the camera on the tripod so that the camera is level and the film plane is parallel with the screen of the video display terminal. Adjust the intensity of the video display terminal so that it is normal or slightly less than normal. You may have to experi-

ment with different intensities, as each video display terminal is different.

**4.** *Exposure.* Turn off all the lights in the room. This prevents reflections on the screen and renders a more accurate photograph. Because screen images have more black in them than illuminated parts, the exposure reading given by your camera probably will be incorrect. The excess black tends to cause the camera's exposure meter to overexpose the photograph. Because each video display terminal is different, you must bracket each exposure at least one stop over and two stops under. For example, if the camera's exposure meter gives you an exposure reading of F/3.5 at 1/30 of a second, you would bracket the exposure by taking a picture at that setting, and also pictures at F/2.8 and F/4.5. If this is the first time you have taken photographs of your video display terminal, you might want to bracket at least one additional stop until you get a feel for the video display terminal you have.

**5.** *Developing.* Have the film developed normally and printed on 8x10-inch, black-and-white glossy paper. This is the standard paper for reproduction use. The printer will reduce the size of the picture for inclusion in your manual.

### Reports
Reports are among the easiest illustrations to do. The simplest way is to print the report on a printer as you normally would when using the program. Just be sure to use white, unlined paper (20-pound weight is best) and use a new ribbon. This gives crisp printouts that can be used full size or reduced by a printer to fit the format of your manual. Printers have a special camera that can photograph and reduce printouts to almost any size.

If your budget is small and you will not be having a printer lay out your manual, you can go to a photocopy shop and have them reduce the report on a reducing photocopier. Be sure the photocopier can produce a clean copy, and don't try to reduce too much, as the readability of the report can be affected.

### Tables and Diagrams
Tables and diagrams can take many forms. The simplest ones can be created on a typewriter or word processor using some of the special character keys such as the hyphen, underline, asterisk, and so on, to create lines, boxes, and whatever you need to create the table or diagram.

If what you need is more complicated, you have two options. First, you can have a printer's art and layout department create your table or diagram from a rough sketch you give them. This is a relatively economical method, as this is just one of the many services they can sell you along with the printing of your manual. However, printers are not always the most creative. Alternatively, you can hire the work out to a freelance commercial artist. While they are more expensive, they usually do the best job. Freelance artists can usually be found in phone books under "Artists," through directories found in many libraries, or by talking to printers who regularly hire artists. You might also consider talking to the head of the art department at a local college or university to see if any student artists are available.

If you can't or don't want to do the tables or diagrams and want to hire the work out, you must be able to tell the artist what you want. During the planning stage you should have decided what was needed and have created a rough sketch of it. This will be the basis for the artist's work.

### Drawings

If you decide to use drawings in your manual, normally you will not be able to do them yourself. This requires that you hire an artist to do them. The least expensive method is to have the artist at your printer (only larger printers will have artists) do them. You should get a good rate as part of the entire printing package. Unfortunately, many of these artists do not have experience in technical drawing.

If you can afford it, try to hire a freelance technical artist as described above. In cities without technical artists, you can settle for commercial artists, who should normally be able to do a good job.

As with tables and diagrams, you will have to provide the artist with a rough sketch of what you need. In some cases, the artist may need to see exactly what is to be drawn. If the artist has never seen a microcomputer and you need a picture of a particular microcomputer, you might have the artist come to your office to do the drawing.

To be sure you will be getting what you need, have the artist do a rough sketch first. Make sure the artist understands your needs. After you approve the rough sketch, have the final drawing made. Ask your printer for the technical specifications of how the drawing should be made. Some drawing techniques lend themselves better to some methods of printing than others.

**Lawford & Associates**

When she was writing the first draft of the manual, Jill used screen dumps of the screen for illustrations. Now that the manual is ready for the printer, she writes out a set of guidelines as to how she wants the illustrations to be handled. These are to be used by the printer and as act as a guide when the printer's art staff designs and creates the illustrations.

**For More Information**

For a brief introduction to the use of illustrations in a technical writing context, see Section 6-6 of *The Elements of Technical Writing* by Joseph A. Alvarez (Harcourt Brace Jovanovich, 1980) or Chapter 12 of *The Complete Guide to Illustration* by Ron S. Blicq (Prentice-Hall, 1982).

For an in-depth examination of illustration techniques, see *The Complete Guide to Illustration and Design,* edited by Terence Dalley (Chartwell Books, 1980). Chapters 1 through 4 cover illustration in general and Chapter 5 is devoted to technical illustration exclusively. The rest of the book is devoted to graphic design.

# 11. Designing Your Manual

Graphic design is the process by which text and illustrations are arranged in your manual so that they clearly communicate with the reader. Good design not only increases clarity, it also makes the manual more interesting to read and ultimately should enhance sales of the software package.

When a customer visits a computer store looking for a good database manager program, he is usually faced with selecting one out of half a dozen or so choices. If he is like the typical customer, he knows nothing about database managers and must make his decision from scanning through the various manuals. He could listen to the advice of a salesperson, but many of them have problems themselves knowing all about the products they carry.

Therefore, the customer starts looking through a manual of a database manager that he has seen advertised. If what he sees is page after page of gray text with few if any divisions or illustrations, and if the manual is 400 or more pages long, he'll be turned off by the manual and look at another. The next one, say, is smaller but contains the same drabness of one gray page after another with no place to rest the eyes.

The third one is different. It starts with a preface that summarizes the software's use. He notices that there are tabbed dividers separating each section, making the manual easy to use. Furthermore, instead of page after page of gray text, he finds the text is broken up with many headings and subheadings and is illustrated with screens, reports, tables, and drawings. This manual will stand out from the others and make an impression. That is what graphic design is all about.

A well-designed manual looks easy to use. Of course if the software itself is of low quality, the manual will not be able to save the package. However, if there are several similar programs and only one has a well-designed manual, that one will probably be the more successful software product.

Unless you are on a tight budget and will be producing your manual on a typewriter or word processor, you will probably leave the design of your manual up to a professional. Like programming or illustration, graphic design is a skill that must be learned over many years. This does not mean you should not be familiar with the principles of graphic design, though. After the basic principles are examined, this chapter will show you one way to design your manual using a word processor (the inexpensive route) and will also tell you how to work with graphic designers, should you decide to hire one, to bring about the best possible manual.

## Principles of Graphic Design

Good manual design follows the principles of unity, sequence, balance, proportion, and emphasis. When considering each of these, remember that the overriding consideration is that design should not intrude on the communication of the manual and should make reading text and understanding illustrations as effortless as possible.

### Unity
The manual's text, illustrations, typeface (the style of type used), white space (any unused portions of a page), and any of the graphic parts of a manual should be consistent and work together as a whole. A cohesive manual offers no surprises to the reader; he always knows what to expect and the manual does not get in the way of his learning the software. Do not use one typeface for some headings and another typeface for others, or use one-inch margins in one section and half-inch margins in another. (See Figure 11-1.)

**Figure 11-1**

*All the graphic parts of a manual must fit together into one cohesive whole so as to not offer any surprises to the user. Inconsistent use of typefaces and margins as illustrated here can confuse the reader and detract from the message you are trying to get across.*

**Tutorial**
Once the program has been prepared, you can begin the tutorial. This section leads you step by step through the use of Home Mortgage Calculator. Not only does the tutorial show you how to use this program, it also gives you practical examples of every operation with the correct results, so you can see how you are doing. The tutorial should not take longer than one-half hour to complete.

Reference Section
*After you have completed the tutorial, you are ready to use Home Mortgage Calculator. However, for additional assistance, should you need it, the reference section contains information about the program arranged in an easy-to-find format. Use the reference section instead of the tutorial to look up*

*operation questions you have
about using Home Mortgage
Calculator once you have become
familiar with it.*

*Appendix*

**In the appendix you will find detailed information on error messages, how Home Mortgage Calculator actually makes its calculations, and a technical discussion about the program. This is optional reading.** *(Most of the appendix is not included.—Ed.)*

### Glossary & Index

The glossary lists many computer-related terms. Use it if you don't understand a term found in this manual. The index provides easy access to information located throughout the manual.

### Quick Reference Card

Accompanying the manual is a quick reference card that summarizes the operation of Home Mortgage Calculator. You may find it easier to use than the manual when you have a simple question about the program's operation.

### Following Examples

Throughout this manual many step-by-step procedures and examples are given. Each of these requires that you type certain commands, eliciting various responses from your computer. To make it easy for you to follow these steps, this manual adheres to the following conventions about keyboard entry and computer responses.

### Entering Commands

Whenever an example is given in this manual, the commands you are to enter via the keyboard will be in all capital letters and indented. Below is an example.

> To start Home Mortgage Calculator, type in the command: HMC after the system prompt and press the: ENTER key to start the program.

---

## Sequence

The order of presentation of material must be logical and consistent. As was discussed in the chapter on organization, the manual should be ordered in logical sections. This also applies at the page level. Each page should read from left to right and top to bottom. Even though this is not the only way to deal with sequence, it is conventional and expected by the reader. Since your goal is to communicate, not to bedazzle the reader, stick to convention. Use headings and graphic devices like bullets to pull the reader from the top of the page to the bottom. Illustrations may be constructed to be read from either left to right or top to bottom, depending on how many there are and what you are trying to get across. (See Figure 11-2.)

**Figure 11-2**

*In the above section from the preface of the Home Mortgage Calculator manual, headings and bullets are used to direct the user to read from the top to the bottom of the page, ensuring that he reads the information in the order that makes the most logical sense.*

# Preface

Welcome to Home Mortgage Calculator.

Home Mortgage Calculator is a computer program designed to help you make informed decisions about home mortgage financing.

With Home Mortgage Calculator you can:

• Calculate any of the following amounts: house purchase price, percentage down payment, loan term, annual interest rate, or monthly mortgage payment.
• See what your monthly mortgage payments would be at various interest rates and purchase prices.
• See what your monthly mortgage payments would be at various interest rates and loan terms.

Home Mortgage Calculator's benefits include:

• It provides the information you need to make informed decisions about home mortgage financing. You no longer have to depend on real estate agents or lending institutions to calculate monthly home mortgage payments for you.
• You can experiment with various combinations of purchase price, down payment, loan term, interest rate, and monthly payment that meet your needs, not the needs of a lending institution.
• Home Mortgage Calculator is easy to use and learn. In less than one hour of practice Home Mortgage Calculator will be working for you.

## Balance

Visually, the text, illustrations, white space, headings, and so on should be balanced on the page so as to be pleasing to the eye. The reader expects a sense of balance and may be distracted by unbalanced pages. This does not mean that two facing pages must be mirror reflections of each other, but rather that one side of a page must not be visually stronger than the other. Do not put three illustrations on the right side of a page and nothing on the left.

## Proportion

Proportion is the visual relationship among such graphics as text, illustrations, white space, and headings. For example, when designing a manual, you could put the same amount of white space around all borders and between all illustrations. Doing this would maintain the same proportion of white space throughout the manual, but it would also be monotonous. Look at any magazine. The amount of white space is varied to add variety to the design and make the pages more visually interesting. However, proportion must also follow the principle of unity, and you can't be reckless in your pursuit of variety. A better way to approach variety in proportion would be to vary the margins on the page level, say a wider margin on the left border of the page than on the right, and to follow this format throughout all the pages of the manual. (See Figure 11-3.)

**Figure 11-3**
*Although even proportions may be easier to design because you don't have to plan as much, uneven proportions make the page more visually interesting.*

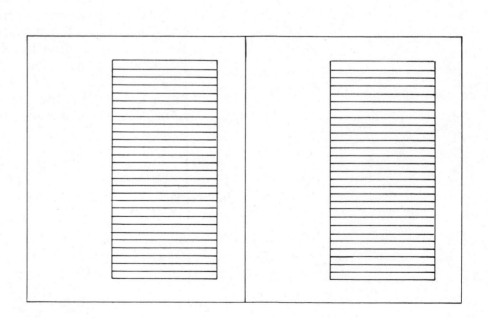

**Emphasis**

Make the most important feature of a page stand out so that the reader knows it is important. Use headings, illustrations, boldface, or other graphic devices to draw attention to important information. Try not to have more than one important feature on a page so as not to confuse the reader. (See Figure 11-4.)

---

**Figure 11-4**

*When you want to bring attention to important points in your text, use graphic devices such as rules to make the information stand out.*

**Loading Home Mortgage Calculator When Your Computer Is Already On**

The second method assumes that your computer is already on and the DOS has been loaded and the system prompt: A› is displayed on your screen. You might use method #2 instead of method #1 if you have completed some other task on your computer and you now want to use Home Mortgage Calculator. This way you don't have to turn your computer off and then on again or do a system reset.

---

Step 1   Insert the working copy of Home Mortgage Calculator in drive A.

---

Step 2   Now type the command: HMC and press the: ENTER key. After about five seconds, Home Mortgage Calculator loads and automatically begins running. You will see the title and copyright screen (Figure 2), and after six seconds, the Home Mortgage Calculator calculator screen will be displayed (Figure 3).

HMC is the name of the program on the Home Mortgage Calculator working copy diskette that starts the program. It may be used at any time to start the program from DOS.

---

All of these principles must work together to bring about good graphic design. One principle should not be emphasized over another. Do not sacrifice good communication for the sake of just trying to follow a principle.

## Who Should Design the Manual?

When it comes time to choose a designer for your manual, you have two choices: yourself or a professional graphic designer. For the best job, the professional (either a freelance graphic designer or one on the printer's staff) is the obvious choice. The professional is trained and may have experience designing user manuals. Hiring a professional is expensive, however, and you may not have the money to spend. If you do it yourself, you will save money but probably will not be able to match the quality of the professional. Some of the reasons for and against designing the manual yourself are:

Reasons for designing the manual yourself—
- Limited publishing budget
- Tight time schedule
- Experienced users
- Limited or specialized market

Reasons for hiring a professional—
- Inexperienced users
- Large market
- Large budget as a result of high expected sales
- No time problem
- Lack of your expertise or desire to do the design

If you have the money and do not have the expertise, definitely go the route of the professional designer. If the software is aimed toward novices and a large market is expected, you need to seriously consider hiring a professional designer, even if you don't think you can afford it. The professional's expertise in communication may mean the difference between success and failure of the software.

On the other hand, if the audience is experienced or the market for the software does not justify the expense of professional design, typesetting, and printing, you can design a satisfactory manual on a word processor.

The next section describes one design method that will meet most of the needs of a well-designed manual. The section after that explains how to work with professional graphic designers.

## Designing the Manual Yourself

There are many ways you can design a manual, but the one discussed here is recommended because it is easy for you to do and results in a manual that is easy for readers to use. It is assumed that you have prepared the manuscript as was described in this book, will format it following the suggestions below, and will reproduce it by the quick-print process. Any other printing process almost demands professional design. See Chapter 12 for further information on printing your manual.

### Equipment
Before you begin, you must have the following equipment and supplies:

*Word Processing Software.* The key to designing and formatting your manual successfully is powerful word processing software. You might be able to duplicate the following format with an electronic typewriter, but it would be time-consuming and frustrating. At the minimum, the word processing software you use should have these features:

- Proportional spacing
- Right-hand text justification
- Heading and footing capability
- Automatic page number capability
- Paragraph margination
- Adjustable left- and right-hand page margination
- Shadow printing (boldface printing)

The more powerful your word processor, the easier it will be for you to format the manual.

*Letter Quality Printer.* While a letter quality printer is not mandatory, it is much preferred over dot matrix printers. The crisp letters produced by a letter quality printer reproduce better and are easier to read. (See Figure 11-5.) If you have to use a dot matrix printer, use only one that has a dense printing head and produces easily readable letters. The letter quality printer should have, at a minimum, these features:

- Proportional spacing
- Microjustification (the ability to vary the white space between letters)
- Shadow printing

If you can afford a fast printer and one that has a tractor feed for use with fan-fold paper, you will save much printing and paper-feeding time.

**Figure 11-5**
*While a letter quality printer is the best choice for the easiest-to-read text, you may not always have access to one.*

```
    Dot matrix printers produce letters that
are made up of many small dots that can some-
times be hard to read.
```

```
    Letter quality printers produce letters that are
fully formed and look as if they were produced by
a typewriter.
```

*Print Wheel.* Use a print wheel whose type is pica (10 characters per inch) and whose style is either Roman or sans serif. (See Figure 11-6.) You probably won't have many choices, but pick a type that is large and appears to be easy to read. The wheel should also be able to print proportional characters.

**Figure 11-6**
*Roman and sans serif are names of two broad classifications of typefaces. Within these classifications are many variations that you can choose from, although you will be limited by what your printer can offer.*

Roman type is very common and has been used for centuries in printing.

Sans serif type has a more modern look and is rapidly gaining popularity as a typeface.

*Carbon Ribbon.* Use a single-strike carbon ribbon with your letter quality printer. It produces sharp, crisp letters which reproduce well during printing. You may go through several ribbons as you print the manual, as single-strike ribbons do not last long. For best reproduction, always use a new ribbon when the manual will be printed on a dot matrix printer.

*Paper.* Use 8x11½-inch, 20-pound, white bond paper. For convenience, use fan-fold paper so that you do not have to load each sheet of paper separately. This size paper is the only convenient size to use with word processors and letter quality printers, and also for quick printing.

## Determining the Format

The actual format of the manual comes next. The format has to do with how the text, illustrations, headings, and white space are arranged on the page. The following suggestions will help you format your manual. You can refine these guidelines to best fit your own needs.

*Margins.* The margins on the left, right, top, and bottom of the paper should measure at least one inch. This use of white space keeps the page from looking crowded and leaves room for the binding on the inner edge of the paper, the heading at the top, and the page number at the bottom.

*Text.* Text (or body copy) should be positioned in one column at the right side of the page, measuring 4½ inches across. It is important to keep the line length of text short to aid ease of reading. The standard 6-inch centered column is hard to read and should be avoided.

*Headings.* Headings should be placed in the 2-inch column at the left of the page, between the left margin and the body copy. Written in uppercase and lowercase, or all uppercase, headings draw attention to the body copy, provide rest spots after long expanses of text, and even can tempt the reader to read on. They should be placed parallel with the start of each section.

*Subheads.* Subheads break larger subjects into smaller, more digestible parts. Place them at the beginning of indented paragraphs and print them in boldface. Make sure that the larger subjects are divisible into two or more subheads, since one subhead by itself serves no purpose. Do not use all caps.

*Titles.* Titles begin new sections and should be right justified, be printed in upper and lowercase, and be boldface. Use titles only to start new sections.

*Running Heads.* A running head (the section title) appears at the top of a page and should be left-hand justified on left-facing pages and right-hand justified on right-facing pages. It should be in normal type and upper and lowercase. The running head changes with each new section. It should not be used for the manual's preface and table of contents.

*Page Numbers.* Page numbers should appear at the bottom of the page. They may be centered, or they may change from the left side to the right depending on whether the page number is odd oreven. Also you have the choice of having the page number appear by itself, like "17," or with the word "page" next to it: "Page 17." Either method works well. Another option is to add the section number to the page number like this: "4-17"; some people find this confusing, however. Page numbers should begin with the first page of the introduction; the preface and table of contents are usually numbered with Roman numerals, such as i, ii, iii, iv, v. . . .

*Illustrations.* Because you are creating and designing the manual yourself, your illustrations will be limited, as we discussed in the previous chapter. Keep all illustration within the 4½-inch column of body copy for consistency. You might want to use the word processor to create the illustrations, or you may want to leave space for the illustrations to be added later.

*Line Height.* Line height, the distance between each line of body copy, is normally established by your word processing software and is commonly ⅙ inch. This is the minimum distance you should use to separate lines of text. Do not try to squeeze more text on a page by reducing the line height. All body copy should be single-spaced. Double spacing does not enhance the readability of text.

**The Design Process**

The design process starts not after the manuscript is written, but during the planning stages of the manual. At this early stage you

Writing Software User Manuals

should try to determine whether you will be designing the manual yourself or having it done professionally. Knowing this will help you to arrange the manual and include the necessary illustrations.

Once the organization of the manual is complete, it is wise to make up a dummy or "mock-up" manual to see roughly how it will look. Include all the manual's sections: title page, copyright page, preface, and so on. You can use either your word processor or paper and pencil to rough out the format. The mock-up does not have to be perfect, but it should outline the important features of the manual. You don't have to include all the pages of the manual, just the first one or two pages of each section, so that you will have a feel for what the finished format will look like. Knowing the format before you write the manual will aid you in the writing and the creating of subsections, important points, illustrations, and so on.

After you have finished the manuscript, you can reformat it to match the specifications of the mock-up format. The reason you do not create the manuscript in the final format is that you will be doing much editing and rewriting and it would constantly have to be reformatted. So type the manuscript with the standard format with heading, subheading, and illustration roughs. Then when you are satisfied with the manuscript, take the time to use the word processor software to reformat the manuscript. A tip: you will find it easier to first format the body copy into the 4½-inch column on each page, then come back and add the headings. It all depends on how your word processor formats text. Experiment to see what works best.

Once the manual is formatted, you can print it so that it is camera-ready for the printer. You might consult the printer before you finish your formatting to see if he has any special requirements not mentioned in this section.

## Having the Manual Professionally Designed

Having the manual professionally designed relieves you of much of the work of publishing a manual. All you have to do is supply the manuscript and rough illustrations to the designer. From there, the design will be made, and then the book will be typeset, laid out, and finally printed. If you decide to go this route, you must also decide who is going to handle the production stages of the manual. You must decide if you will hire a freelance graphic designer or have the printer design the manual.

### Choosing a Designer

The least expensive way to have your manual designed is to make the designing a part of the printing package offered by the printer. Often, this service includes the design, the typesetting, the finished illustrations, layout and paste-up, and the printing and binding. Going the package route ensures consistency, reduced time and effort, and less cost. To have the best job, you must go to a full-service printer (many printers do not offer all of the above services) and find one who has worked with instruction manuals before. You may not be able to find such a printer and may have no choice but to hire a freelance graphic designer to design the manual.

If you can find a freelance graphic designer who specializes in technical publications, you will be much better off than using the design services of a printer. Freelancers often are better trained and have more flexibility over their work. While the design will normally be better, your cost will be larger. As the design is not part of a package price, you will be paying the freelancer by the hour. Also, since different people are doing the design and the printing, you will have to deal with more people, coordinating their work, and this may involve more time.

You can find a freelance graphics designer by asking for recommendations from a printer, looking in the yellow pages of the phone book (Artists—Commercial), and getting directories of freelancers from libraries or associations.

### Working with the Designer

A good working relationship with the designer, whether freelance or on staff, helps to ensure that the manual's design will be appropriate and meet the needs of your readers. The first thing you must do is learn the language of graphic design. This chapter should help greatly, but like computer programmers, designers have their own jargon. If a designer ever uses a term you do not understand, be sure to have it explained, or you might end up getting something you do not expect.

When you first discuss with the designer what you need, you will want to include the following subjects.

*Budget.* Tell the designer how much you can afford to spend, both for his services, and for the printing of the book. Different designs can significantly affect the cost of the manual, both in printing and binding.

*Designer's Familiarity with Computer Software.* Even the best designer needs to understand what computer software is and how readers use software manuals to learn how to use it. If the designer does not have computer experience, it is a good idea to have him sit down in front of a microcomputer with the software and manual manuscript to go through it. This will help the designer know what is involved.

*Marketing Considerations.* It is a good idea to discuss marketing factors to be considered in the sale of the software. If you are not the marketing expert, then whoever is should come to the meeting to discuss his point of view. Although you do not want marketing aspects to interfere with the manual's ability to communicate, the designer needs to know how to blend in the design of the manual with whatever packaging and advertising are planned.

Writing Software User Manuals

## What the Designer Does

After you sit down with the designer and discuss your needs, and after researching the subject, the designer will determine the following:

- Page size, type of paper
- Margin size, measured in points
- Width of body copy, measured in points
- Type style, size, and weight for body copy and headings
- Amount of leading (space between lines)
- Arrangement of illustrations
- Cover design (if not handled by marketing department of publisher)

Once all of these factors are determined, the designer will produce a dummy of the manual showing how everything fits into place. Look it over to see if it seems to fit your needs. It is your prerogative to ask why certain things are done and to suggest changes. If changes are required, then a new dummy will be prepared, although of course these changes may cost extra.

At this point the designer's job is done. The design specifications are given to the typesetter and the layout artist for execution of the design. The designer might be the same person as the layout artist. This is especially true if you have a printer design and lay out the manual.

## Business Relationship

As in any business transaction, you should treat your relationship with the designer as you would that with any business partner. Looking for the best price (maybe taking bids) is all a part of publishing a manual. And don't forget the contract. Even though the relationship may not be long, get a contract specifying exact responsibilities and costs. Otherwise you may find that you are paying far more than you expected.

**Lawford & Associates**

When Jill first negotiated her contract with David, they agreed that the manual design would be done by the printer, following guidelines provided by Jill. The agreement was the result of a compromise between the two after a heated discussion.

"Jill, I'm a small software publisher, competing with thousands of other publishers for the same market. My budget is tight and I can't afford to hire a freelance graphic designer. That's what I'm hiring you to do. If you can write the manual, you can surely design it. What can be so difficult about it?"

"I can't design the manual just as I can't design and write Home Mortgage Calculator. Graphic design is a separate skill apart from writing and my training in it is next to nothing."

"Maybe I should hire a writer who has been trained in design. It would save me a lot of money." There is a short pause.

"You said that you're competing against thousands of other publishers. Right?"

"That's right. And I have to be careful where I spend my money."

"I agree. It's because you are small and have a lot of competition that I am recommending you hire a professional designer. If you want Home Mortgage Calculator to stand out from the rest, it must be professionally designed. Go into any computer store and look at the manuals. Most are terrible because they have not been professionally done. Even though your budget is tight, what you do spend is going to be wasted if the manual is not done right."

"I appreciate what you're saying, Jill, but that still doesn't mean I can afford it. I have only so many resources. I almost wrote the manual myself to save money, but the last time I did that the software didn't sell well. Of course it may not have been the manual's fault. MICROSOFT came out with a similar product two weeks after I released mine."

"I know how to settle this. Instead of hiring a freelance designer, what if we have the printer do the design. Many of the full-service printers provide graphic design services. If I provide them with some guidelines, they should do a better job than I would. And it won't cost a great deal. When I put out the bid for the printing, I'll include the design and layout services. Most printers provide design as a service and make their money from their printing. What do you think?"

"Okay. But only if the cost isn't too high. When you put out the bids, have the design costs separated from everything else so I can see how much extra it will cost me. If it's too high, then you'll do the design. Fair enough?"

"Do I have a choice?"

**For More Information**  If you want to learn more about graphic design, try these books.

*The Complete Guide to Illustration and Design,* edited by Terence Dalley (QED Publishing, 1980) and *The Graphics Handbook,* by Howard Munce (North Light Publishers, 1982) provide a general introduction to basic graphic design.

For a more comprehensive discussion, try *Publication Design,* by Roy Paul Nelson (Wm. C. Brown Co., 1983). It includes an in-depth look at art, design, and typography.

# 12. Printing Your Manual

Would you buy a television without a cabinet? A car without a paint job? A book without a cover? Of course you wouldn't. And if you are like most people, the type of cabinet, paint job, or cover influences the television, car, and book you buy.

The same holds true for buyers of software packages. They want the software package to be visually appealing. Many buyers associate an attractive package with quality contents. This means that a software user manual's printing and binding must also be inviting. This is not an absolute rule, since some buyers' needs will always transcend a manual's packaging, but this is infrequently so. It is the superficial packaging more than the content that often determines which software package is chosen.

This does not mean that a manual's printing has to be done on slick, glossy paper with color photographs of sexy models pointing out the features of the program's operation. Or that the manual has to be bound in cloth or leather. The key word in all of the above is *inviting*, not elaborate. Even inexpensively printed and bound manuals can be inviting to pick up and use, and producing an inviting product should be your goal. Expensively packaged manuals won't be successful if the information they are meant to communicate is lacking in clarity.

This chapter is devoted to the various aspects of printing and binding your manual. How much you spend is dependent on the budget and marketing decisions. The options and methods are examined below.

## Types of Printers

There are many types of printers offering a variety of printing and binding services. Your first contact with printers is apt to be bewildering. Like computer programmers, they use a language all their own, and they offer many options of printing methods, types of paper and ink, and degrees of service. This section will discuss only the basic information you need to have about printing and binding user manuals.

Essentially, there are three types of printing shops you can deal with. While there are exceptions to these categories, most of the printers you see listed in the yellow pages of your phone book include:

**Photocopy Shops.** These specialize in reproducing documents of all types using xerography, a photocopying process that uses electrical charges to transfer images. They can copy on one or both sides of a piece of paper, reduce or enlarge a document, and even collate, or assemble, small documents. For a limited number of copies, usually less than 100, they are inexpensive and fast. On the other hand, the reproduced quality is often inconsistent, one time being sharp and another time giving dirty copies, and their reproduction of photographs is poor.

*Never* have final versions of user manuals printed at photocopy shops. Their inability to produce consistently high-quality copies, their relative high cost (for quantity duplication), and the lack of flexibility in paper size all result in uninviting manuals. For preliminary, in-house, or test manuals where speed is important, quantity is small, and quality of printing is not important, photocopy shops serve you well, but this is the only instance where they are acceptable.

**Quick-Print Shops.** These specialize in using an electrostatic offset reproduction process, where a special type of photograph is taken of the document to be duplicated. You provide the printer with a camera-ready document, either printed with a dot matrix or letter quality printer (formatted and ready to go), or typeset (pasted up and ready to go). Besides offering quick printing services, most of these printers offer typesetting, proofreading, paste-up, collating, and binding services. As a sideline, most quick-print shops also offer photocopy services.

**Full-Service Shops.** Besides offering photocopy and quick-print services, the full-service shop offers more sophisticated methods of offset printing using metal plates and ink instead of electrostatic offset printing. These methods also give you the ability to print in two or more colors. As in quick printing, a special photograph is taken of the camera-ready pages. Unlike the case with quick printing, where dot matrix or letter quality printing and formatting are acceptable, only pasted-up typeset pages work well. Besides advanced printing capability, full-service shops usually offer design, illustration, typesetting, proofreading, paste-up, collating, and binding services.

**Deciding How to Print and Bind Your Manual**

You have to make the following decisions in regard to the printing and binding of your manual.

- Whether to design and print the manual yourself or to have the manual professionally designed, typeset, and printed.
- Whether to have the manual quick-printed or printed using the metal plate offset process.
- Whether to bind the manual with a spiral binding or like a loose-leaf notebook.

Each of these options is discussed below along with some recommendations.

### Self-Designed and Printed vs. Typeset

Your budget probably will be the largest factor in deciding whether to design and print the camera-ready manual yourself or to have the manual professionally designed, typeset, and pasted up. Budget should not be your only consideration, however. The various advantages and disadvantages of each method are discussed below.

**Self-Designed and Printed.** Essentially, this includes writing the manuscript in standard manuscript format, then, using the format suggested in Chapter 11, reformatting the manuscript on your word processor and then printing it with a dot matrix or letter quality printer. Ideally, you should use a letter quality printer, an easy-to-read typeface, and single-strike, black carbon ribbon on good quality paper. Doing this produces camera-ready pages ready to be photographed for quick printing. Pros and cons of doing this yourself include:

**Pros:**

**1.** It's relatively inexpensive. You should already have the necessary equipment, so all you need to do is take the time to prepare the camera-ready pages.

**2.** It's fast. You do everything yourself, on your own schedule, and do not have to wait for a printer to perform the camera-ready preparation services.

**3.** You control all aspects of formatting, proofreading, and printing of the camera-ready pages and have absolute control over how the final products look, within the limits of your equipment.

**Cons:**

**1.** Printed pages are not as professional looking as typeset pages.

**2.** You have fewer choices in format, typeface style and size, headings, and so on.

**3.** You have fewer choices of page size.

**4.** There are fewer types of illustrations that can be used.

**Professionally Typeset.** If you decide to have your manual professionally designed, typeset, and pasted up, you will turn the polished manuscript over to the typesetter to enter the text into a typesetting machine, which electro-optically, using a microprocessor, forms the images of the text on special film; the film in turn produces a print of the text which is used to produce the camera-ready pages. This job is usually hired out entirely. All you do is hand over the manuscript, and everything else is done by the printer.

Typeset pages can be used either for quick printing or metal plate offset printing. The pros and cons of typesetting your manual include:

**Pros:**

1. A typeset manual is professional looking and is expected by most readers.
2. You have a larger choice of format, typeface style and size, headings, and so on, each making the manual easier to read and more graphically interesting.
3. You have more choices of page size.

**Cons:**

1. Typesetting is an expensive process.
2. It's time-consuming. You are at the mercy of the printer and have to wait for him to complete the work at his pace.
3. Typesetting also requires that the manual be designed and pasted up—two additional expenses.

**Typesetting Yourself.** This is one option you might consider if your budget is tight but you want to typeset your manual. Many printing firms are offering the ability either to accept text over the phone lines or to use text stored on floppy diskettes, and typeset it without having to rekey it. Keying time is one of the largest expenses of having a manual typeset.

For this method to work, the text has to be somewhat modified by insertion of proper commands to the typesetting machine so that it knows the various characteristics of the text to be printed. Some firms alter the text for you, and others let you enter the proper commands, following their instructions. This last method gives you the largest time and money savings.

After the text is typeset by the printer, the galley proof, a copy of the typeset text, is returned to you for proofreading. You can then either paste it up yourself or give it to the printer to paste up. As with all production methods, there are some pros and cons of this you must know about.

**Pros:**

1. It's less expensive than conventional typesetting, saving as much as 50 percent or more of the cost of having the printer do all the work.
2. You control the typesetting and get exactly what you want.

**Cons:**

1. As most of the firms specializing in computerized typesetting are concentrated in large cities, you may have a small time delay in receiving the galley proof.
2. If corrections have to be made, additional mailing time delays may occur.
3. You have to learn how to use the typesetting commands. While usually not difficult, it does take some time.

**Quick Copy vs. Metal Plate Offset**

If you decide to format and print your own camera-ready manual, you have little choice but to use quick copy printing. However, if you typeset your manual, you have the choice of either quick copy or metal plate offset printing. The advantages and disadvantages of each are described below.

**Quick Copy** If you use quick copy printing, the printer will take your camera-ready pages and print them to your specifications. Pros and cons of this method include:

**Pros:**
1. It's inexpensive. For quantities of 50 to 1,000, this is one of the least expensive ways to print a manual. The type of paper you choose will significantly affect your cost. You will have to select page size, weight, color, and texture, and some of these options can more than double the bill for the paper.
2. It's fast. In most cases, you can have your manual printed in one or two days, depending on the length of the manual and the number of copies you need.
3. The text does not have to be typeset.

**Cons:**
1. Reproduction quality is not professional looking, but it's adequate.
2. Photographs cannot be reproduced adequately, although line drawings can be.

**Metal Plate Offset.** As with quick copy, the printer uses camera-ready pages to print the manual according to your specifications. However, instead of an electrostatic method, metal plates and ink are used to print the manual. Pros and cons of this method include:

**Pros:**
1. Printing quality is professional looking.
2. Photographs can be reproduced well.
3. It's economical for long press runs, over 1,000 copies.

**Cons:**
1. It's expensive. Because typeset text and paste-up are required, the overall cost of this method is more expensive than going the self-designing and printing route for camera-ready pages and quick printing.
2. It's time-consuming. The entire process from typesetting, to paste-up, to printing may take several weeks or more, depending on the size of the manual.

### Choosing a Binding

No matter how you decide to print your manual, you have two good choices for binding it. There are more than two ways to bind a manual, but the spiral and loose-leaf binding methods lend themselves best to user manuals. Actually, more important than the look of the binding is how well the manual lies open for use in front of a computer.

Almost all users will go through the manual's tutorial while in front of their computer, so the binding must allow the manual to lie flat. The spiral and loose-leaf methods are the two best ways to achieve this. Most full-service printers should be able to provide you with either method of binding.

**Spiral Binding.** A spiral binding, either plastic or metal, allows the manual to lie flat, no matter to what page it is opened. Almost all printers offer the plastic binding; the metal spiral binding may be harder to find. You will also have to have front and back covers printed, usually on a heavy cardboard stock. In many cases, the design of the cover will be decided by the marketing people (or owner) of the software publisher and you will be responsible only for seeing that correct design gets on the cover. In some cases, you might be responsible for hiring out the design work; if so, handle this as you would the rest of the design of the manual (see Chapter 11). Pros and cons of using spiral bindings include:

**Pros:**
1. Plastic bindings are the least expensive, with metal spiral bindings close behind.
2. The manual always lies flat.

**Cons:**
1. Extra pages (or correction pages) cannot be inserted should the manual need minor updates or changes.
2. Plastic bindings are not especially professional looking.

**Loose-Leaf Binding.** All full-service printers will be able to drill the holes necessary for the pages to be inserted in the loose-leaf binder. Some printers will be able to provide printed binders of many different types and qualities, whereas others can only recommend a binding company specializing in bindings. You can take the expensive route and have custom-made cloth binders with holders, or go the cheaper route and use off-the-shelf binders that can have a label attached to them. This decision will have to be made on the basis of your budget and marketing plans. The pros of using loose-leaf binding include:

**Pros:**
1. If you choose quality custom-made binders, the result is a very professional looking binding.
2. The manual lies well.
3. It is easy to insert pages as needed.

## Making a Decision
If you are having difficulty deciding which printing and binding route to take, here are some guidelines that may help you.

**Self-Designed and Printed and Quick Copy.** The combination of creating your own camera-ready pages and quick copy printing should be used when:
1. Your budget is tight.
2. The market for your software and manual is small and you expect to print fewer than 1,000 copies.
3. You have a need for fast turnaround in printing.
4. The potential users or buyers are experienced computer users.
5. You have no need to use photographs.

**Typeset and Quick Copy.** The combination of having the manual typeset, pasted up, and quick-copy printed should be used when:
1. You have a low to medium printing budget.
2. The market for your software and manual is small and you expect to print fewer than 1,000 copies.
3. You expect either novice or experienced users.
4. You have no need to use photographs.

**Typeset and Metal Plate Offset.** The combination of having the manual typeset, pasted up, and metal plate offset printed should be used when:
1. You have a medium to large printing budget.
2. The market for your software and manual is large and you expect to print more than 1,000 copies.
3. You expect either novice or experienced users.
4. You have a need to use photographs.
5. Time is not critical.

**Spiral Bindings.** You should use a spiral binding when:
1. You have a small to medium size budget.
2. You don't expect to update the manual regularly.
3. You don't feel you have to compete with similar products that have fancy bindings.

## Loose-Leaf Bindings.
You should use a loose-leaf binding when:
1. You have a medium to large size budget.
2. You expect to update the manual regularly.
3. You feel you have to have a fancy binding to compete with similar type products.

## Business Matters

The relationship between the manual writer and the printer is a business one and should be handled in a professional manner. Do not deal with the first printer you run across in the yellow pages. Talk to three or four printers, finding out their capabilities. Once you have found two or three you think can meet your needs, have them bid for the entire printing job, however you define it. You will be surprised at how much difference there can be between the bids. Do not necessarily go with the lowest bid, but take into consideration the printer's reputation and the time frame in which the printing can be completed.

Don't try to skimp on your budget by trying to print some copies now with the possibility of printing more in three months when more are needed. Doing this may be tempting, but it is very expensive in the long run. For example, the per manual cost of having 2,000 copies printed may be half the cost of having 1,000 printed. You have to weigh the costs of paying for manuals now at a lesser cost, and paying later at a higher cost; be sure you get all the facts by having the printer's bid include a variety of quantities so you can make a sound decision.

Once all the bids are made and you have selected a printer, be sure to have a contract drawn up specifying exactly what the printer offers to do at what cost, and what is expected of you. This prevents any possible problems later.

Try to develop a good working relationship with the printer. Know which individuals you must contact to answer any questions if they arise, and try to work with them and learn all you can about their job. The better you understand what they do and how they do it, the better your manual will be.

## Lawford & Associates

Now that the software and manual are ready for publication, Jill prepares a bid form and gives it to six full-service printers she previously talked to and feels can do a good job. She includes with each bid form the specifications for the manual design so that the printers will have some basis on which to make accurate bids. Jill gives the printers one week to complete their bids, as David wants the manual printed as soon as possible.

At the end of the week she receives four bids and carefully examines them, comparing the costs and the estimated completion dates, and weighing in her mind the reputation of each printer.

The lowest bidder, Newhart Quality Printing, is 8 percent lower than the next lowest bidder; however, the estimated completion date is four weeks and she remembers that a friend told her they are not easy to work with and often miss their completion dates. Also, she learned in a previous discussion with them that they have never designed or printed a manual before.

The next lowest bidder, Bombay Printing Service, while never having printed a user manual before, has designed and printed training manuals for a local vocational school. Jill has seen the manuals and is impressed with their work. The only problem is that they cannot have the manuals done until four weeks from now.

The other two bidders submitted almost identical bids, about 6 percent higher than Bombay Printing Service. The biggest advantage with both of them is that they claim to be able to do the manuals within two weeks.

Jill knows by now that David would go with the lowest bidder, Newhart Quality Printing, even if there is a time delay. What worries her is their lack of experience. So to make the decision easy for David, she tears up the bid for Newhart Quality Printing.

During her next Monday meeting with David she gives him the three bids and, as Jill expected, he gives her the go-ahead to have Bombay Printing Service do the job.

The same afternoon, Jill brings the manuscript to Bombay and gives them the job. Since she had the bid figures, she has drawn up a contract and has the printer sign it. Jill and the sales representative agree that when the design is complete, she will approve it. Also, she will proofread and check the typeset galley proofs and the final pasted-up page proofs when they are complete. This way Jill remains in control of the quality of the manual. With this task out of her way, Jill is ready to go about getting the manual copyrighted.

**For More Information**

If you want to learn more about typesetting your manual yourself, order a copy of *A Guide to Personal Publishing* from Intergraphics, Inc., 106-A South Columbus Street, Alexandria, VA 22314. Write beforehand to find out the cost. Intergraphics is a firm specializing in self-typesetting, and their 122-page book shows you everything you would want to know about doing your own typesetting. There are even chapters on design and paste-up, and charts showing dozens of typefaces and various type sizes. Even if you decide not to use Intergraphics' services, this manual is well worth its small cost because of its wealth of information.

# 13. Copyrighting Your Manual

You're not finished with the manual yet. It's true that the hard part is over, but you still must take the time to copyright the manual. This is not as complicated as it may seem and it's an important step to protect your manual from infringement.

A copyright is a legal right given to the author of an original work (in your case, a manual), to control its reproduction and distribution. This protection begins at the time the manual is actually written and lasts the lifetime of the author plus 50 years. With works for hire (where you hire out your writing services or are an employee of a firm, and the firm retains the copyright) and for works copyrighted by a company, the life of the copyright lasts 75 years from publication of the manual, or 100 years from the time of the manual's creation, whichever is shorter. Should anyone impinge on your rights during this time, you may sue for damages.

Though it is not required, you should register your copyright with the United States Copyright Office. This is a legal formality that ensures you complete protection of your manual. You may register the copyright of either an unpublished or published manual. According to the publication "Copyright Basics," published by the Copyright Office, you receive these benefits when you register your copyright:

• Registration establishes a public record of the copyright claim.
• Registration is ordinarily necessary before any infringement suits may be filed in court.
• If made before or within five years of publication, registration will establish prima facie evidence in court of the validity of the copyright and of the facts stated in the certificate.
• If registration is made within three months after publication of the work or prior to an infringement of the work, statutory damages and attorney's fees will be available to the copyright owner in court actions. Otherwise, only an award of actual damages and profits lost is available to the copyright owner.

While registering your copyright with the United States Copyright Office protects your copyright in this country, it does not necessarily protect it in other countries. Most countries, including the United States, are members of the Universal Copyright Convention (UCC), and while these countries usually recognize a copyright from another country, the nature of the protection varies. If you intend to sell the software and manual in other countries, it is wise to contact each country (or an attorney specializing in international copyright) before publication of the manual to see if there are any special registration requirements.

**Who Owns the Copyright?** Although the ownership of a manual originally belongs to the author of a work, the author of the work is not always the creator of the work. Sound confusing? Here is how "Copyright Basics" explains this apparent dilemma:

> The copyright in the work of authorship *immediately* becomes the property of the author who created it. Only the author or those deriving their rights through the author can rightfully claim copyright.
>
> In the case of works made for hire, the employer and not the employee is presumptively considered the author. Section 101 of the copyright statute defines a "work made for hire" as:
>
> 1. a work prepared by an employee within the scope of his or her employment; or
> 2. a work specially order or commissioned for use . . . as an instructional text . . . if the parties expressly agree in a written instrument signed by them that the work shall be considered a work made for hire. . . .
>
> The authors of a joint work are co-owners of the copyright in the work, unless there is an agreement to the contrary.

This section of the copyright law has significant implications for the authors of software manuals. If you are an independent programmer writing your own manual to accompany your software, the law is clear. Because you are not working for someone else, you can register the copyright of the software manual in your own name. The only exception would be if you signed a contract with someone stating explicitly that the software was commissioned for him and that the job was a work-for-hire agreement. In this case, you would give up the copyright of the manual (and the software).

If you are a freelance writer contracted to write a software manual, the copyright of the manual would belong to you unless the contract you signed explicitly stated that the job was a work-for-hire agreement. This is why it is so important to get a signed contract and not rely on just a gentleman's agreement or a handshake. In most cases, though, the party commissioning the work will require that the job be a work-for-hire agreement.

If you are a staff manual writer for a software publisher, the copyright automatically belongs to your employer and you have no recourse to gaining ownership of the copyright.

In any of these cases, the fact that you are not the copyright owner does not mean you cannot file the copyright registration in the name of the copyright owner. One of your responsibilities as a manual writer may be to file the registration for its owner.

## The Copyright Notice

As the manual writer, you are also responsible for ensuring that the copyright notice appears on all copies of the published manual. Copyright law states that this notice must appear if you want to retain all of your legal rights.

Normally, the copyright notice appears on the manual's copyright page (see Chapter 4) and takes the form of:

**1.** The symbol © (the letter "C" in a circle), or the abbreviation "Copr.," or the word "Copyright."

**2.** The first year of the manual's publication.

**3.** The name of the copyright owner.

Some examples of copyright notices include:

© 1984 David Lawford

Copr. 1984 Lawford & Associates

Copyright 1984 D. Lawford

Unpublished Work © 1984 Lawford & Associates

The first three copyright notices are variations of the same copyright and are legal to use. In each of these cases, the manual is published. The fourth example is of a copyright notice of an unpublished work. Though this notice is not required on unpublished manuals, it is suggested in order to prevent accidentally publishing a manual without the copyright notice. As you write your manual, this type of copyright notice should appear on all drafts of the manuscript. Use the current year of writing as the year in the notice.

## Registering the Copyright

To register your copyright, you must either:

Write:  Register of Copyrights
       Copyright Office
       Library of Congress
       Washington, D.C. 20559

or

Call:  (202) 287-9100 any time, day or night, and
     leave a recorded message.

Request several copies of Form TX (never use a copy of the form, only an official original copy), which is used to register the copyrights of published and unpublished nondramatic literary works— another way of saying a software manual. After you receive the forms, fill out one form per manual to be registered and mail it with a check, draft, or money order for $10; enclose two copies of the best edition of the published manual, or one copy of an unpublished manual. Mail the package to the address listed above, where you got the registration forms. After about 90 days you will receive the copyright registration certificate from the Copyright Office.

**Lawford & Associates**

Even though Jill signed a work-for-hire agreement with Lawford & Associates and does not own the copyright of the Home Mortgage Calculator Manual, one of her contractual jobs is to complete the copyright registration. Dave knows little about these matters and feels that Jill, as a freelance writer, is the expert.

In the planning stages of the manual, Jill wrote the Copyright Office and inquired about the copyright procedure. She had always left the copyright registration to her publishers before, so she had to learn the proper steps for herself. When she received the information, during the outlining stage, she called the Copyright Office phone number and requested three copies of form TX. She wanted extra copies in case she should accidentally make a mistake in filling out the form. She knew that only official forms are accepted by the Register of Copyrights.

As she did not need the forms for some time yet, she filed them but did take the suggestion of the pamphlet "Copyright Basics" and placed a copyright notice on all of her drafts of the manual as she proceeded. The notice "Unpublished Work Copr. 1984 Lawford & Associates" was placed at the beginning of the manuscript draft in the word processing file and was printed every time the file was printed.

Now that the completed manuscript is being prepared for printing, Jill decides to go ahead and register the copyright before the manual is published, as her contract will expire as soon as the printing is completed. She carefully reads the instructions that came with form TX and proceeds to fill out the form. (See Figure 13-1.)

After filling out the form, Jill has Dave approve it and she mails it, making this the last official act of writing the manual for Home Mortgage Calculator.

**For More Information**

For a brief but clear introduction to the subject of copyrights, write for "Copyright Basics" by the U.S. Copyright Office. It is a good primer that will answer most of your questions about copyrights and copyright registration. The Copyright Office also offers a circular called "Publications of the Copyright Office," which lists all the free publications about many aspects of the copyright law. Both publications are free and may be obtained from:

Information & Publications Section
LM-455
Copyright Office
Library of Congress
Washington, D.C. 20559

# FORM TX
## UNITED STATES COPYRIGHT OFFICE

REGISTRATION NUMBER

_____

TX _____ TXU _____

EFFECTIVE DATE OF REGISTRATION

_____

Month _____ Day _____ Year _____

**DO NOT WRITE ABOVE THIS LINE. IF YOU NEED MORE SPACE, USE A SEPARATE CONTINUATION SHEET.**

## 1

**TITLE OF THIS WORK** ▼

HOME MORTGAGE CALCULATOR USER MANUAL

**PREVIOUS OR ALTERNATIVE TITLES** ▼

**PUBLICATION AS A CONTRIBUTION** If this work was published as a contribution to a periodical, serial, or collection, give information about the collective work in which the contribution appeared. **Title of Collective Work** ▼

If published in a periodical or serial give: **Volume** ▼     **Number** ▼     **Issue Date** ▼     **On Pages** ▼

## 2

**a**   **NAME OF AUTHOR** ▼

Lawford & Associates

**DATES OF BIRTH AND DEATH**
Year Born ▼     Year Died ▼

Was this contribution to the work a "work made for hire"?
☒ Yes
☐ No

**AUTHOR'S NATIONALITY OR DOMICILE**
Name of Country
OR { Citizen of ▶ _____
Domiciled in ▶ U.S.A. _____

**WAS THIS AUTHOR'S CONTRIBUTION TO THE WORK**
Anonymous? ☐ Yes ☒ No
Pseudonymous? ☐ Yes ☒ No
If the answer to either of these questions is "Yes," see detailed instructions.

**NATURE OF AUTHORSHIP** Entire text   Briefly describe nature of the material created by this author in which copyright is claimed. ▼

**NOTE**

Under the law, the "author" of a "work made for hire" is generally the employer, not the employee (see instructions). For any part of this work that was "made for hire" check "Yes" in the space provided, give the employer (or other person for whom the work was prepared) as "Author" of that part, and leave the space for dates of birth and death blank.

**b**   **NAME OF AUTHOR** ▼

**DATES OF BIRTH AND DEATH**
Year Born ▼     Year Died ▼

Was this contribution to the work a "work made for hire"?
☐ Yes
☐ No

**AUTHOR'S NATIONALITY OR DOMICILE**
Name of country
OR { Citizen of ▶ _____
Domiciled in ▶ _____

**WAS THIS AUTHOR'S CONTRIBUTION TO THE WORK**
Anonymous? ☐ Yes ☐ No
Pseudonymous? ☐ Yes ☐ No
If the answer to either of these questions is "Yes," see detailed instructions.

**NATURE OF AUTHORSHIP** Briefly describe nature of the material created by this author in which copyright is claimed. ▼

**c**   **NAME OF AUTHOR** ▼

**DATES OF BIRTH AND DEATH**
Year Born ▼     Year Died ▼

Was this contribution to the work a "work made for hire"?
☐ Yes
☐ No

**AUTHOR'S NATIONALITY OR DOMICILE**
Name of Country
OR { Citizen of ▶ _____
Domiciled in ▶ _____

**WAS THIS AUTHOR'S CONTRIBUTION TO THE WORK**
Anonymous? ☐ Yes ☐ No
Pseudonymous? ☐ Yes ☐ No
If the answer to either of these questions is "Yes," see detailed instructions.

**NATURE OF AUTHORSHIP** Briefly describe nature of the material created by this author in which copyright is claimed. ▼

## 3

**YEAR IN WHICH CREATION OF THIS WORK WAS COMPLETED** This information must be given in all cases.
1984 ◄ Year

**DATE AND NATION OF FIRST PUBLICATION OF THIS PARTICULAR WORK**
Complete this information ONLY if this work has been published.
Month ▶ _____ Day ▶ _____ Year ▶ _____ ◄ Nation

## 4

**COPYRIGHT CLAIMANT(S)** Name and address must be given even if the claimant is the same as the author given in space 2.▼

Lawford & Associates
1234 Main St.
Springfield MO  65801

See instructions before completing this space.

**TRANSFER** If the claimant(s) named here in space 4 are different from the author(s) named in space 2, give a brief statement of how the claimant(s) obtained ownership of the copyright.▼

**DO NOT WRITE HERE OFFICE USE ONLY**

APPLICATION RECEIVED

ONE DEPOSIT RECEIVED

TWO DEPOSITS RECEIVED

REMITTANCE NUMBER AND DATE

**MORE ON BACK ▶**
• Complete all applicable spaces (numbers 5-11) on the reverse side of this page.
• See detailed instructions.
• Sign the form at line 10.

**DO NOT WRITE HERE**

Page 1 of _____ pages

EXAMINED BY _____

CHECKED BY _____

☐ CORRESPONDENCE Yes

☐ DEPOSIT ACCOUNT FUNDS USED

FOR COPYRIGHT OFFICE USE ONLY

**DO NOT WRITE ABOVE THIS LINE. IF YOU NEED MORE SPACE, USE A SEPARATE CONTINUATION SHEET.**

**PREVIOUS REGISTRATION** Has registration for this work, or for an earlier version of this work, already been made in the Copyright Office?

☐ Yes ☒ No If your answer is "Yes," why is another registration being sought? (Check appropriate box) ▼

☐ This is the first published edition of a work previously registered in unpublished form.

☐ This is the first application submitted by this author as copyright claimant.

☐ This is a changed version of the work, as shown by space 6 on this application.

If your answer is "Yes," give: **Previous Registration Number** ▼ _____ **Year of Registration** ▼ _____

**5**

**DERIVATIVE WORK OR COMPILATION** Complete both space 6a & 6b for a derivative work; complete only 6b for a compilation.

**a. Preexisting Material** Identify any preexisting work or works that this work is based on or incorporates. ▼

**b. Material Added to This Work** Give a brief, general statement of the material that has been added to this work and in which copyright is claimed. ▼

**6**

See instructions before completing this space.

**MANUFACTURERS AND LOCATIONS** If this is a published work consisting preponderantly of nondramatic literary material in English, the law may require that the copies be manufactured in the United States or Canada for full protection. If so, the names of the manufacturers who performed certain processes, and the places where these processes were performed **must** be given. See instructions for details.

**Names of Manufacturers** ▼ _____ **Places of Manufacture** ▼ _____

**7**

**REPRODUCTION FOR USE OF BLIND OR PHYSICALLY HANDICAPPED INDIVIDUALS** A signature on this form at space 10, and a check in one of the boxes here in space 8, constitutes a non-exclusive grant of permission to the Library of Congress to reproduce and distribute solely for the blind and physically handicapped and under the conditions and limitations prescribed by the regulations of the Copyright Office: (1) copies of the work identified in space 1 of this application in Braille (or similar tactile symbols); or (2) phonorecords embodying a fixation of a reading of that work; or (3) both.

a ☒ Copies and Phonorecords   b ☐ Copies Only   c ☐ Phonorecords Only

**8**

See instructions.

**DEPOSIT ACCOUNT** If the registration fee is to be charged to a Deposit Account established in the Copyright Office, give name and number of Account.

**Name** ▼ _____ **Account Number** ▼ _____

**9**

**CORRESPONDENCE** Give name and address to which correspondence about this application should be sent. Name/Address/Apt/City/State/Zip ▼

Jill Bates, Lawford & Associates
1234 Main St.
Springfield, MO 65801

Area Code & Telephone Number ▶ (417) 555 4567

Be sure to give your daytime phone ◀ number.

**CERTIFICATION\*** I, the undersigned, hereby certify that I am the

Check one ▶
☐ author
☐ other copyright claimant
☐ owner of exclusive right(s)
☐ authorized agent of Lawford & Associates

of the work identified in this application and that the statements made by me in this application are correct to the best of my knowledge.

Name of author or other copyright claimant, or owner of exclusive right(s) ▲

**Typed or printed name and date** ▼ If this is a published work, this date must be the same as or later than the date of publication given in space 3.

Jill Bates

April 1, 1984

date ▶

Handwritten signature (X) ▼

*Jill Bates*

**10**

**MAIL CERTIFI-CATE TO**

**Certificate will be mailed in window envelope**

Name ▼
Jill Bates, Lawford & Associates

Number/Street/Apartment Number ▼
1234 Main St.

City/State/ZIP ▼
Springfield, MO 65801

**Have you:**
• Completed all necessary spaces?
• Signed your application in space 10?
• Enclosed check or money order for $10 payable to *Register of Copyrights*?
• Enclosed your deposit material with the application and fee?

**MAIL TO:** Register of Copyrights, Library of Congress, Washington, D.C. 20559.

**11**

\* 17 U.S.C. § 506(e): Any person who knowingly makes a false representation of a material fact in the application for copyright registration provided for by section 409, or in any written statement filed in connection with the application, shall be fined not more than $2,500.

☆ U.S. GOVERNMENT PRINTING OFFICE: 1982-361-278/58

Sept. 1982—600,000

# 14. Freelance Manual Writing

Freelancers of all professions enjoy being their own bosses. What other kind of job allows you to do what you want, when you want, and how you want, all while getting paid? Many manual writers are freelancers: either freelance programmers writing their own manuals, or freelance writers practicing their skill in a burgeoning new market for good writing. If you are called by either of these pursuits, here are some tips to strengthen your business acumen.

**The Freelance Programmer as Manual Writer**

A freelance programmer may work only part-time, squeezing in time to write programs during evenings and weekends while holding down a full-time job. Or the freelance programmer may have given up the security of working for someone else and gone into full-time freelancing, living on his programming and business skills.

Typically, the freelance programmer first comes up with an idea for a better way to do a task with a computer. Maybe no other software exists, so a completely new market is opened up; maybe he just has come up with a better way of doing something that has been done before. After the idea is set in his mind, he outlines his plan for the program. He may spend as much as half the total time of the project on the planning before he begins to write the program. After he completes the writing stage, he tests the program for errors, corrects them, and makes other refinements and improvements.

He still is not done, however. If he wants to sell his program to a software publisher, or even publish it himself, he will have to come up with program documentation and a user manual. The program documentation, or the instructions relating directly to the design and operation of the program itself, should have been written during the planning, programming, and final testing of the program. If the programmer has been lax in maintaining proper documentation during the writing of the program, this task must be completed before the program is sent to a software publisher. Having incomplete or nonexistent program documentation is a sure way not to sell a program.

The program's user manual can be approached in two different ways. Either the freelance programmer can turn out a complete user manual, as outlined in this book, or he can provide an abbreviated manual, perhaps consisting only of the "Getting Started" and "Reference Sections," and let the software publisher use this as a basis for writing the finished user manual. Whichever decision the freelance programmer makes may significantly affect the eventual success or failure of his program.

## Why Freelance Programmers Should Write Their Own User Manuals

If at all possible, freelance programmers should try to write the complete user manual for their software. Here's why.

• As a freelance programmer, you have complete control over the manual, thus ensuring that it is done well and accurately. You can leave the final design and editing to the software publisher—you are not an expert in everything—but at least you know some unknown technical writer will not butcher the manual, rendering it useless.

• Submitting a complete user manual to a publisher along with your software increases the likelihood that your program will be published. Publishers do not always have the time or money to write a good manual. They are more likely to buy software from a programmer who includes a manual than from a programmer who submits a program without a complete manual. Also, the inclusion of a manual tells the publisher you care enough about your program to do it right, further reinforcing the impression that you are a professional. Of course, there is the occasional publisher who will not even consider your submission unless a complete manual is included. If this is the case, you have no choice but to write your own manual.

• Some software publishers pay freelance programmers a higher royalty if they have written a complete manual. The publisher will be saving time and money and will often reward programmers for their efforts. Even if the publisher does not offer more money, you can try to use the complete manual as a negotiating tool to improve the terms of your contract. It can't hurt to try.

• If the freelance programmer is really ambitious, he may want to market the software package himself. As the publisher, the freelance programmer has absolute control over the product, along with all the profits that accrue with being the programmer, manual writer, and publisher. While the profits can be high, however, marketing your own software is risky and requires the programmer to be a jack-of-all-trades. Many people don't feel comfortable doing everything whereas others relish the thought.

## Why Freelance Programmers Should Not Write Their Own Manuals

Even though ideally freelance programmers should write their own user manuals, there are still a number of good reasons why they should not. They are:

• Some people just do not like to write. They may be able to write well enough to get by, but they find it tedious and just do not want to do it. If freelance programmers are willing to give up some money, that is their prerogative.

• Some programmers feel that they can make more money by programming than by writing a manual. It's a matter of which is a more profitable way for them to spend their time. Not writing the manual may reduce the potential profits, but even more profits might be lost by a programmer's not having the chance to spend time writing another program. Only the freelance programmer knows which route is best for him.

• Probably the best reason for a freelance programmer not to write his own user manual is that he simply can't write. Unfortunately, many programmers have an inadequate background in writing and are not interested in trying to improve their skills. If this is the case, the programmer should definitely not write his own manual, but rather should seriously consider collaborating with a professional writer.

## What Freelance Programmers Must Know Before They Write Their Manual

If you are a freelance programmer and have decided to write your own user manuals, you need to be aware of two major mistakes made by programmers. The first, and perhaps worse, mistake is not considering who the audience for the manual is. The second is using excessive computer-related technical terms and jargon. Both of these subjects are covered in this book, but some extra emphasis here can't hurt.

While you may think you know who your audience is, you must not forget that many people may be using the program who are not included in your prospective audience, and these people probably do not have any computer experience. Play it safe by assuming that computer novices will be using your program. Try to put yourself in the place of a beginner and ask yourself what should be included. If you have difficulty being objective, find three or four computer novices and have them test the manual to see if they can understand it. The earlier in the manual writing stage that you do such testing, the further ahead you will be.

Technical terms scare beginning readers away and should be avoided, or at least defined the first time they are used. This mistake is easier to avoid than is the mistake regarding your audience, but often it's neglected because of laziness. If you have trouble finding nontechnical terms, use a computer dictionary and a thesaurus to help you find the most understandable definitions. Guidelines are also offered in this book.

If you follow the suggestions in this book and take special care to define your audience and write at their level, you should have few problems writing a good user manual. It does take time and hard work, but it may mean the difference between the success or failure of your software.

## Collaborating with Freelance Writers

You don't always have to submit a complete manual with your software, but the advantages of doing so are great. If you decide not to write the manual yourself, for whatever reason, you should consider collaborating with a freelance writer.

There are three reasons why you should consider such a collaboration: (1) you are freed of the responsibility of writing and can devote your time to programming instead; (2) it ensures that your manual will be written well and helps to ensure that your software will be bought by a software publisher; and (3) planning the manual when planning the program usually results in both a better program and manual; waiting to write the manual after the program is written usually results in a poorer manual.

Another option is to hire a freelance writer or editor to edit your manual after you have written it. This is less expensive than having it completely freelance written and ensures that your manual will be professionally done.

It is best to start the relationship with the freelance writer at the very beginning, when the program is being planned. Find a freelance writer through your own contacts, the yellow pages (under Writers—Freelance), or classified advertising in computer publications, or you can advertise in a local paper or computer publication or even get listed in a directory such as *Writer's Market*. If you have seen the work of a local writer, use the white pages to call him and see if he is available. After meeting with the writer and discussing your needs—and finding out if the writer can do what you want (give him this book to read if he has not written user manuals before)—work together to plan the software and manual, planning step by step everything that needs to be done. The writer should be able to aid you in designing screens that communicate clearly and are consistent with the manual.

Be sure to get a contract specifying the writer's exact responsibility and how he will be reimbursed. The least expensive way to hire the writer is to share the royalties earned from the sales of the program. This way you do not have to put any of your own money up front. You may have to share as much as 25 to 50 percent of your royalties, however, as the writer will be taking a large risk that the program will even sell. Alternatively, you can pay the writer an hourly or a fixed fee. You will have to negotiate the financial arrangements that work best for the both of you.

Having the manual written by a professional writer should increase the chances of your software's being bought by a publisher, and you should mention this fact when you submit the software and manual package.

If you should decide to self-publish the software and you are not a polished writer, you must seriously consider having the manual either completely freelance written or at least edited by a professional writer. As a publisher, you won't have the luxury of having someone else review the manual—you're on your own. Any errors or problems with the manual will directly affect the success of your software.

## The Freelance Writer as Manual Writer

Freelance writers make their living as professional communicators. In the day-to-day work of freelance writers, they might write an article, edit a newsletter, research a book, or even write a speech. While most freelancers write any kind of nonfiction, most specialize in areas that interest them. As with freelance programmers, their livelihood depends on their professional and business skills. One of the newest opportunities for freelance writers is writing about computers, especially in the form of software user manuals.

### What Kind of Work Can Freelance Writers Expect?
As a freelance writer, there are three principal types of manual writing work you can do. They are:
• You can write the manual from scratch, starting with the planning of the software, thus ensuring consistency between the software and the manual.
• You can edit and rewrite a user manual written by the program author or someone else. This could involve a major rewrite that might take as long as writing a manual from scratch, or it might require only minor copy editing and refinement. Most often you will have to rewrite the manual, slanting it toward the intended audience and removing the jargon.
• If your communications skills also include graphic design and layout and paste-up skills, you may be able to write, design, and lay out the entire manual as a complete service.

As the software industry is still new and dynamic, you must keep aware of any possible opportunities that may arise as the industry changes. Subscribing to several trade journals such as *Infoworld* or *Computer Retail News* is one way to keep up.

### Where to Find Freelance Writing Jobs
Jobs as freelance manual writers may be found in two major areas: in collaboration with freelance programmers, and with software publishers.

The best way for inexperienced manual writers to get started is to find freelance programmers, who, like you, have to submit their work to publishers to be accepted. User manuals are integral parts of freelance programmers' submissions and are the area many programmers are weakest in.

Locate freelance programmers through friends, by talking with computer store personnel, and by advertising in local newspapers or computer magazines. Have business cards printed emphasizing that you specialize in computers, and distribute them at local computer group meetings, fairs and trade shows. Tell likely clients that you are a writer and want to know if you can write a professional manual to accompany their software. If they are not familiar with the benefits of good manuals, tell them. Also tell them that you have read this book and that you can write a good manual. If this will be your first user manual, offer to write the manual on speculation for a cut of the royalties and, if possible, a portion of the advance, if the programmer gets one. Or, if you can negotiate it, try to get paid by the hour or by the job—whatever best fits your needs.

After you reach an agreement with the programmer, be sure you sign a contract specifying exactly what your responsibilities are, the timetable for completion of your duties, and your pay. A contract is just one more indication that you are a professional writer.

If you are more experienced, you should consider working as a freelance (or maybe even on the staff) for a software publisher. Software houses buy freelance software and often have to write and edit manuals for it. Also many firms develop software in-house and require manuals to be written.

The best way to contact software publishers for freelance work is to send them a cover letter indicating your interest, along with your resume and related writing samples. If you have written user manuals before, include a copy. It helps to live in the same vicinity as the publisher, but you don't have to be in the same town. If you do live in the same area, consider calling ahead and making an appointment with the owner or manager of the software house. Some larger publishers have their own publishing group; if so, you would want to contact the group manager.

If you land a freelance job with a software publisher, you will probably be paid by the hour, sometimes by the job. Just as with freelance programmers, get a signed contract specifying all your responsibilities, the time schedule, and money.

**What You Have to Know to Write Software Manuals**
Reading this book, and knowing how to write to communicate is all you have to know to write user manuals. Don't worry about knowing anything about computers when you start, though you will probably become an expert once you have written your first manual.

Being a computer novice gives you an edge in being objective about the manual so that you write it from the perspective of the beginner. You must be willing to learn about computers and get to know the program whose manual you are writing inside and out. Don't think you can write the manual without learning about computers along the way.

Another consideration in writing software manuals is that you must have the software and the computer that it works on available for use. This may mean that you must borrow the computer from the freelance programmer or software publisher, or must go to their respective offices to work. Of course you may want to buy your own computer. Not only will this give you a computer to operate the software on, you can write the manual on the computer using word processing software. Even if you do borrow a computer or use the one at the office, buying your own personal computer can give you an advantage in all of your writing.

The opportunities for freelance writers in the computer industry are diverse and constantly growing. If you are thinking of an area to specialize in or just want to increase your writing income, writing for the computer industry can be satisfying and exciting, especially if you like to work at the edge of technology. Writing software user manuals is just the first step to entering the whole world of computer-related writing. Hundreds of computer magazines and books are currently being published. You might as well take part in this latest bonanza. If you're already an accomplished writer, you have a distinct advantage over most of the people now submitting material to these markets. Learn what you can about computers, and editors will be seeking you out for assignments.

# Glossary

**Accounting system.** One or more computer programs that work together and maintain accounting records for an organization. May include the general ledger, accounts receivable, accounts payable, inventory, order entry, and personnel records.

**Application.** A specific user need to be fulfilled, such as bookkeeping or tax preparation in a business.

**Application software.** A computer program that is designed to solve a particular user demand, such as a word processor for writing or a game for entertainment.

**ASCII.** An acronym for the American Standard Code for Information Interchange. This is a special format used by most microcomputers to represent alphanumeric characters.

**Assembly language.** A low-level programming language that uses symbolic instructions to represent each action performed by a central processing unit (CPU).

**Audience.** The people who use a particular program or read a particular software user manual.

**Backup.** The procedure to make a duplicate copy of a program or data diskette.

**Beta-testing.** The process by which a computer program is tested in a real-life situation before it is published.

**Body copy.** The actual text, or written words, that make up any written work, such as a user manual.

**Bracket.** A photographic term that means to make a number of different exposures of the same subject (such as a video display screen) under the same lighting conditions, to ensure a correct exposure.

**Breadth.** Refers to how broadly a subject is covered, the extent of a subject's scope.

**Bugs.** Errors in a computer program.

**Bullets.** Graphical devices, such as circles, dots, or stars, that are used to bring important points or information to the attention of the reader.

**Camera-ready.** Refers to text and artwork that has been specially prepared so that it can be reproduced.

**Command.** An instruction that is given to a computer program by a user and that is usually typed in, not chosen from a menu.

**Contact sheet.** A special photograph—created by light passing through negatives onto a sheet of photographic paper—that shows the pictures you took on a roll of film. It's used to determine which pictures are suitable for enlargement.

**Copy.** Written material, such as the text found in a user manual.

**Copyright infringement warning.** A written warning, usually found on the copyright page of a user manual, that warns users that it is against the law to copy the user manual in any form without permission of the copyright owner.

**Copyright notice.** A notice, required by law, that must appear on all published copyrighted works. Usually found in the form of: "© 1984 John Doe."

**Customer service information.** Information—such as name, address, and phone number—that tells users where they can find additional information about a program.

**Database.** Usually considered an applications program used to store and retrieve similar-type information, such as a mailing list.

**Data entry.** The process by which a user enters data into a program for processing or manipulation by the program.

**Depth.** Refers to how deeply a subject is covered, how many details are included about a subject.

**Disk drive.** The physical hardware that is used to store and retrieve data from a diskette.

**Diskette.** A flexible magnetic disk used to store either a computer program or data.

**Disk operating system.** A program that controls the entire operation of the computer. It is always running in a computer that is on.

**Disk preparation.** A procedure whereby a diskette is formatted for use for the first time.

**DOS.** An abbreviation for *disk operating system.*

**Electronic spreadsheet.** An application program that allows users to create financial models.

**Entry.** An item that is entered. A user *enters* a piece of data into a program.

**Examples.** Practical samples that illustrate, in detail, a particular point. Usually found in user manuals to show how to perform a certain task or procedure.

**Exercises.** Problems or tasks that are designed to increase the skill of a user. Usually found in user manuals to give users additional practice in procedures.

**File.** An organized collection of information, such as a program or data.

**Galley proof.** A trial sheet that shows what typeset text looks like. It's usually used to find errors and make corrections.

**Graphic design.** The arrangement or composition of text and graphics on a page.

**Graphics designer.** The person who creates the graphic design of a user manual or other book.

**Hacker.** Computer jargon for a person who is very devoted to programming and using computers.

**Hardware.** The physical equipment that makes up a computer.

**In-house.** Refers to something done from within, such as when a software publisher hires a manual writer full-time to write manuals for the firm's software.

**Integrated.** A combination of separate program functions that work together as one.

**Jargon.** Terminology (slang) unique to a particular profession.

**Justified.** Refers to the alignment of text on a piece of paper such as all flush left or flush right.

**K.** An abbreviation for *kilobyte*. One kilobyte equals 1,024 bytes.

**Keyboard commands.** Commands that are given to a computer program via a computer keyboard, such as by pressing the *Enter* key.

**Layout.** The process by which someone designs and pastes up a camera-ready page.

**Leading.** The amount of space between two lines of text.

**Line drawing.** A drawing created only from lines, such as a cartoon.

**Main menu.** The most important or most used menu in a program.

**Manual content.** The actual technical information found in a manual that describes to the user how to operate the program.

**Manual organization.** The arrangement of necessary operating information about a software product into a functional, orderly whole.

**Manuscript.** A written document.

**Marketing research.** Usually, a formally conducted investigation on the product needs of consumers. For example, a survey might be conducted to see what kinds of software are currently desired by users but are not presently being published.

**Menu.** A list of choices from which the user can select an action to be performed by a program.

**Menu-driven.** A program whose operation is controlled by the user completely through menu choices.

**Microjustification.** The ability of a printer to adjust the amount of space between characters of text. It is used to create text that is right-justified.

**Offset.** A type of printing that transfers an image from one flat surface to another.

**Organizational elements.** These are the main sections, or parts of a manual, that organize the manual into logical units of related information. The title page, copyright page, preface, table of contents, introduction, getting started, tutorial, reference section, appendix, glossary, index, and quick reference card are all considered organizational elements.

**Outline.** A formal plan, usually quite detailed, that describes how a manual is to be written and what is to be included.

**Paste-up.** The process by which camera-ready artwork or copy is prepared for the printer.

**Pica.** A size of a typeface that permits ten characters to the inch.

**Point size.** A unit of measurement for type size. There are 72 points to the inch.

**Printer driver.** A part of a computer program that transfers output from a program to a printer.

**Program.** A set of instructions, written in a programming language, that tells a computer what to do.

**Program documentation.** The written record of how a program works. Usually includes a flowchart and an annotated source code listing.

**Programmer.** A person trained to write computer programs.

**Programming language.** A human-like language that is used to tell a computer what to do and how to do it.

**Proportional spacing.** The variations in spacing between the characters of printed text so that the amount of horizontal space for each letter or number is proportional to its width.

**Prose.** Ordinary writing, such as that found in user manuals.

**Quick Reference Card.** Usually a small card or folder that has printed instructions on how to operate a computer program.

**Report.** Usually a printout generated on a computer printer by a computer program.

**Roman typeface.** A family of typefaces that typically have thick and thin strokes along with serifs.

**Sans serif typeface.** A family of typefaces that typically have strokes of equal thickness and don't have serifs.

**Screen.** The text or graphics that appears on a video display screen at a particular time.

**Screen dump.** A process by which the contents of a video display screen are reproduced on paper by a printer.

**Shadow printing.** The same as boldface printing.

**Slant.** The approach as to how you write a manual to appeal to a specific audience.

**Software.** Another term for a computer program.

**Software package.** Usually includes the program on diskette, the user manual, and the physical packaging used to contain the two.

**Start-up procedure.** Before many programs can be used, the user must go through a series of steps to get the computer and program ready. These actual steps are the start-up procedure.

**Statement.** Usually a comment or instruction found in a program line.

**Structured programming.** Refers to a formal and disciplined approach to planning and writing a computer program.

**Style sheet.** Usually a self-made list of writing style rules and guidelines that you write down to ensure consistency in your writing.

**Support.** Refers to the amount of help or assistance software publishers or retail computer store dealers provide users once they have sold a software package to them.

**Target.** The means by which you alter your writing to meet the needs of a particular audience.

**Text file.** A computer file that contains text, usually in the ASCII format. Manuscripts stored by a word processing program are stored in text files.

**Tutorial.** A step-by-step method to teach a user how to use a computer program.

**Typeface.** A particular style of type.

**Typesetting.** The process by which type is set by an electro-optical machine into camera-ready copy.

**User.** A person who uses a computer program.

**User manual.** Written instructions on how to operate a computer program.

**White space.** Any unused portion of a page.

**Word processor.** An application program used by anyone who wants to create, edit, and format text with a computer.

**Working copy.** A copy of a program diskette employed in everyday use. This is used instead of the original program diskette so that in case it is damaged or destroyed, you always have the original.

**Work-for-hire.** Usually contracted work done by a writer, who gives up the ownership of what he writes.

**Writing style.** This is the unique way you select words to communicate in your writing.

**Xerography.** A photocopying process that uses electrical charges to transfer images.

# INDEX

## A

Advertising, 2
After-sale support, reduction of, 2
Appendix, 35
Application knowledge, of user, 15-16, 17-18, 19-20
Artists, freelance, 116, 118-119. *See also* Graphic designer, freelance
Audience, 14-20
  application knowledge of, 15-16, 17-18
  beginner, 17, 18
  computer experience of, 15, 17
  expert, 17, 18
  intermediate, 17, 18
  knowledge of, 16, 152
  program needs of, 16
  researching, 15-16
  slanting manual to, 14, 16-18
    outline and, 40
    reference section and, 71, 72
    tutorial and, 58-59
  user error by, 16

## B

Beta-testing, 77, 79
Bids, 133, 142
Binding, 136
  loose-leaf, 140, 141
  spiral, 140, 141
Budget, establishing, 10

## C

Completion dates. *See* Schedule
Computer experience
  of user, 15, 17, 19
Content of manual
  breadth of, 14, 17, 18
  depth of, 14, 17
Contracts
  with freelance graphic designer, 133
  with freelance writer, 153, 155
  sample of, 6
Copyright, 144-149
  definition of, 144
  ownership of, 145
  registering, 146
    benefits of, 144
    Form TX, 146, 148-149

"Copyright basics," 144, 145, 147
Copyright notice, 146
Copyright page
  contents of, 23-24
  guidelines for writing, 25
  purpose of, 23-25
  use of, 23
Customer satisfaction, 2, 26

## D

Design. *See* Graphic design
Diagrams, illustration of, 115, 118-119
Drawings, illustration of, 116, 119

## E

Equipment. *See also* Hardware; Software; Word processor
  graphic design, 130-131
  listing necessary, 33, 34
Error messages,
  user handling of, 33. *See also* User error
Examples
  instructions for following, 31
  proper use of, 51
  in reference section, 71
  testing of, 74
  in tutorials, 60, 65
  writing, 75
Exercises
  testing of, 74
  in tutorials, 61, 64, 65
  writing, 75

## F

Freelance graphic designer, 131-133
Freelance manual writer, 150-156
  freelance programmer as, 150-54
    advantages of, 151
    collaboration of, with freelance writers, 153-154
    disadvantages of, 151-52
    mistakes to be avoided by, 152
  freelance writers as, 154-156
    job opportunities for, 154-155
    knowledge requirements for, 155-156

Freelance programmers, as writers, 3.
  *See also* Programmers
Freelance writers, 3
  contract with, 153
  finding, 153
  as manual writers, 154-156
  programmers collaboration with, 153-154

## G

Getting started section
  benefits of, 33
  guidelines for writing, 34
  purpose of, 33
  use of, 33
Glossary, 157-161
  benefits of, 36
  purpose of, 35
  use of, 36
  writing of, 36
Goal setting, 8-10, 11
Graphic design, 121-135
  bullets, 124
  consistency in, 122
  format for, 129-130
  of headings, 124, 126, 129-130
  of illustrations, 130
  line length, 130
  of margins, 129
  of page numbers, 130
  principles of, 122-126
    balance, 125
    emphasis, 126
    proportion, 125
    sequencing, 124
    unity, 122-123
  by professional, 131-133
    reasons for, 127
  references for, 134
  of running heads, 130
  of subheads, 130
  of text, 129
  of titles, 130
  typefaces, 126
  white space, 125
  on word processor, 122, 128-129
  by writer, 127-131
    design process, 130-131
    equipment, 127-129
    reasons for, 127
  in tutorial, 61
Graphic designer, freelance
  bids from, 133
  choosing, 131-132
  contract with, 133
  interview questions, 132
  responsibilities of, 133
  working with, 132

## H

Hardware, 33, 34, 74. *See also* Word

processor
"Home Mortgage Calculator User Manual," 81-111

## I

Illustrations, 75, 112-120
  diagrams, 115, 118-119
  drawings, 116, 119
  graphic design of, 124, 125, 130
  guidelines for creating, 112-113
  planning of, 117
  purpose of, 112
  in reference section, 71
  references for, 119-120
  reports, 114, 118
  screens, 113-114
    photographic procedures for, 117-119
    template procedures for, 117
  supplies for, 74
  tables, 115, 118-119
  in tutorials, 60, 61, 63
Illustrators, 116, 118-119
Index, 36-37
  benefits of, 36
  purpose of, 36
  use of, 36
  writing guidelines for, 36-37
Introduction, 31-33
  benefits of, 31
  contents of, 31-33
  purpose of, 31
  use of, 31

## K

Keyboard commands, explanation of, 32-33

## M

Market, 2-3
"Mock-up" manual, 131

## O

Objectives, setting of, 8-10
Organization of manual, 21-39
  benefits of, 22
  characteristics of
    balance, 21
    consistency, 21-22
    logic, 21
    relevance, 21
    sequence, 21
  elements of, 22-38
    appendix, 35
    copyright page, 23-25
    getting started, 33-34
    glossary, 35-36
    index, 36-37
    introduction, 31-33
    preface, 26-27

quick reference card, 37
reference section, 34-35
table of contents, 28-30
title page, 23, 24
tutorial, 34
Outline, 39-45, 73-74
drafting, 41-42
on index cards, 41
on word processor, 41
guidelines for, 42
importance of, 39-40
preliminary research for, 40-41
for reference section, 71
sample of, 43-45
Overview
benefits of, 32
in introduction, 32
in preface, 26
in tutorial section, 60-61

**P**

Photography, use of, 115, 117-118
Planning process, 3, 7-13
as cooperative effort, 7-10
goals/objectives in, 8-10, 11
Preface
benefits of, 26
contents of, 26
guidelines for writing, 26, 26-27
purpose of, 26
use of, 26
Printers, 118
bids from, 142
contract with, 142
full-service shops, 136
photocopy shops, 135-136
quick-print shops, 136
Printing, 135-143. *See also* Binding;
   Printers
metal plate offset, 139, 141
quick copy, 139, 141
references for, 143
self-designed and printed, 137, 141
typeset, 141
Printing package, 131
Program, writer's use of, 11, 40-41
Program control, 32-33
Program documentation, reading, 10-
   11
Programmers
cooperating with, 7-8, 10-11
interviewing of, 40-41
as writers, 3, 150-154
Proofreading, 79
Publishing. *See* Printing

**Q**

Quick reference card, 37

**R**

Reference section, 34-35, 66-72
benefits of, 35
format of, 67-70
   dictionary-style, 67-68
   encyclopedia-style, 69-70
   modified encyclopedia-style, 69
guidelines for writing, 71
inclusion of, 35, 66-67
purpose of, 34, 66
sequencing in, 21
user experience and, 17, 18
Reports, illustration of, 115, 118
Reviews, magazine, 2, 72
Rewriting, guidelines for, 76-77

**S**

Sales objectives, 9
manual designs and, 2
Schedule, establishing, 10
Screens, illustration of, 114-115, 117-
   118
Software, 33, 34, 74
beta-testing of, 77
Style sheet, 54, 55, 79

**T**

Table of contents, 28-30
benefits of, 28
contents of, 28
guidelines for writing, 28-30
inclusion of, 28
purpose of, 28
standard, 28, 29
summary, 28-29, 30
Tables, illustration of, 115, 116, 118-119
Templates, 117
Terminology
definition of, 32
explanation of, 35
Testing methods, 77-78
Title page, 23, 24
Tutorial, 34, 57-66
benefits of, 34
definition of, 57
guidelines for writing, 59-60
inclusion of, 34, 57-58
purpose of, 34, 57
sequencing in, 21
user experience and, 17, 18, 58-59
Tutorial segments
exercises, 61, 64
hands-on-practice, 61, 62-64
introduction, 60, 62
overview, 60-61, 62
summary, 61, 64
Typesetting. *See* Printing

## U

User confidence, building, 33
User errors,
  consequences of, 16, 20

## W

Word processor
  carbon ribbons for, 129
  graphic design with, 122, 128-129
  outlining on, 41, 43
  paper for, 129
  print wheel for, 128-129
  printer for, 128
  references for, 79-80
  rewriting on, 76-77
  software for, 74, 128
  for tables and diagrams, 118
  writing on, 74-75
Work-for-hire agreements, 145, 147
Writers, types of, 3. *See also* Freelance
      manual writer; Freelance writers
Writer's block, 39, 73
Writing process, 73-80. *See also* Outline
  first draft, 74-76
  polishing, 78
  preparatory requirements, 73-74
    illustration supplies, 74
    microcomputer and software, 74
    outline, 73-74
    word processing software, 74

proofreading, 79
rewriting, 76-77
testing, 77-78
Writing style, 46-56
  abbreviations, 49, 53, 55
  analogies, 51
  capitalization, 53, 55
  clarity of, 1, 9-10
  cliches, 49
  comparisons, 51-52
  consistency in, 53-54, 71
  establishing point, 46-47
  examples, 51
  good vs. poor, 46
  grammar, 54, 55
  initials, 49
  jargon, 48-49, 55, 152
  metaphors, 51
  numbers, 55
  overused words, 49
  pace, fast vs. slow, 50-51
  punctuation, 55
  references for, 55-56
  similes, 51
  symbols, 49
  tense, 53
  tone, 52
  voice, active vs. passive, 52-53
  word choice, 47-49
  wordiness, 49-50

# Other Books Of Interest

**Art/Music**
  Artist's Market, $14.95
  Making Money Making Music, by James Dearing $12.95, paper
  Performing Artist's Handbook, by Janice Papolos $15.95
  Songwriter's Market, $13.95

**Photography**
  Developing the Creative Edge in Photography, by Bert Eifer $16.95, paper
  How to Create Super Slide Shows, by E. Burt Close $10.95, paper
  How You Can Make $25,000 a Year with Your Camera, by Larry Cribb $9.95, paper
  Photographer's Market, $14.95
  Sell & Re-Sell Your Photos, by Rohn Engh $14.95
  Starting—And Succeeding In—Your Own Photography Business, by Jeanne Thwaites $18.95
  Wildlife & Nature Photographer's Field Guide, by Michael Freeman, $14.95

**Lifestyle**
  Clutter's Last Stand, by Don Aslett $8.95, paper
  Confessions of an Organized Housewife, by Deniece Schofield $6.95, paper
  Do I Dust or Vacuum First?, by Don Aslett $6.95, paper
  How to Hold Your Audience with Humor: A Guide to More Effective Speaking, by Gene Perret $13.95
  Is There Life After Housework?, by Don Aslett $6.95, paper
  Partnering: A Guide to Co-Owning Anything from Homes to Home Computers, by Lois Rosenthal $12.95, paper

**Travel/Employment**
  Internships, $10.95, paper
  Summer Employment Directory of the U.S., $8.95, paper
  Work Your Way Around the World, $10.95, paper

**Writing**
  Beginning Writer's Answer Book, edited by Polking and Bloss $14.95
  Complete Guide to Greeting Card Writing, edited by Larry Sandman $7.95, paper
  Complete Guide to Writing Nonfiction, edited by Glen Evans $24.95
  Complete Guide to Writing Software User Manuals, by Brad McGehee $14.95, paper
  Fiction Is Folks: How to Create Unforgettable Characters, by Robert Newton Peck $11.95
  Fiction Writer's Market, $17.95
  Freelance Jobs for Writers, edited by Kirk Polking $7.95, paper
  Getting the Words Right: How to Revise, Edit, and Rewrite, by Theodore A. Rees Cheney $13.95
  How to Become a Bestselling Author, by Stan Corwin $14.95
  How to Write a Cookbook and Get It Published, by Sara Pitzer, $15.95
  How to Write a Play, by Raymond Hull $13.95
  How to Write Short Stories that Sell, by Louise Boggess $7.95
  How You Can Make $20,000 a Year Writing, by Nancy Hanson $6.95, paper
  Make Every Word Count, by Gary Provost $7.95, paper
  Programmer's Market, edited by Brad M. McGehee $16.95, paper
  Travel Writer's Handbook, by Louise Zobel $8.95, paper
  Writer's Encyclopedia, edited by Kirk Polking $19.95
  Writer's Market, $18.95
  Writer's Resource Guide, edited by Bernadine Clark $16.95
  Writing From the Inside Out, by Charlotte Edwards $9.95, paper

To order directly from the publisher, include $1.50 postage and handling for 1 book and 50¢ for each additional book. Allow 30 days for delivery.

**Writer's Digest Books, Dept. B, 9933 Alliance Rd., Cincinnati OH 45242**
Prices subject to change without notice.